IMAGES OF THE
GREEK THEATRE

RICHARD GREEN
ERIC HANDLEY

IMAGES OF THE GREEK THEATRE

University of Texas Press
Austin

International Standard Book Number 0-292-72782-8
Library of Congress Catalog Card Number 94-61639
Copyright © 1995 The Trustees of the British Museum

First University of Texas Press edition, 1995
All rights reserved
Printed and bound in Spain

Requests for permission to reproduce material from this work
should be sent to Permissions, University of Texas Press,
Box 7819, Austin, Texas 78713-7819

Designed by John Hawkins

Front cover: Storming party: the lover with the ladder. Paestan red-figure bell-krater
attributed to Asteas, soon after the middle of the 4th century BC. See fig. 31.

Frontispiece: Orestes takes refuge at Delphi. Paestan red-figure bell-krater by Python,
c. 350–340 BC. See fig. 24.

Contents

But pardon, gentles all,
The flat unraisèd spirits, that have dared,
On this unworthy scaffold, to bring forth
So great an object. Can this cockpit hold
The vasty fields of France? Or may we cram
Within this wooden O the very casques
That did affright the air at Agincourt?

SHAKESPEARE, *Henry V*, Prologue

Acknowledgements

It is a pleasure to recall here the generous support we have received for the work on which this book depends, both from institutions, with finance and hospitality, and from friends and colleagues in various ways. We should like to thank the Australian Research Council and the University of Sydney; the National Humanities Center, North Carolina, and its Director, Professor W. Robert Connor; and the Master and Fellows of Trinity College, Cambridge. For all that modern communications can do (we have exchanged faxes that make up a file many times larger than the finished product), the chance to be under the same roof for a while, at the NHC in 1992 and in Trinity in 1993, is something with a value of its own. When the organising of text and photographs is in question, our gratitude goes to Carolyn Jones, Joanna Champness and the staff of British Museum Press, and to Dr D. J. R. Williams and his colleagues in the Department of Greek and Roman Antiquities at the Museum, where most of the objects we illustrate are housed. Other Departments of the Museum, and other authorities at home and abroad have in their turn been helpful in providing material for illustrations and permission to use it; for help with proof corrections (though without implicating our colleagues in such waywardnesses as survive) we thank Professor P. E. Easterling and Dr Neil Hopkinson; and for special help of one kind or another, we thank Sir John Boardman, Professor Lilly Kahil, Dr D. Peppas-Delmousou, Dr Robert Robson and Mr R. W. Sword. Our long-term indebtedness to T. B. L. Webster and to A. D. Trendall, both personally and to their writings, may or may not be plain to anyone coming fresh to this subject; it is nevertheless very deep.

March 1994   J.R.G.
                                                                              E.W.H.

CHAPTER 1

Seeing and Hearing

The Greek for theatre is *theatron*, a place for seeing something. The word survives in modern languages, not least Greek itself, as a sign of the deep roots of the theatrical traditions of our own world, and perhaps also of the ways in which those traditions still bear fruit. The design of the National Theatre in London took part of its inspiration from a building well over two thousand years older, at Epidauros in Greece; the National Theatre was still quite new when Aeschylus' *Oresteia* was produced there in 1981, and was seen by many more thousands of people on television. One could multiply examples from many places in different countries of modern productions of ancient Greek plays, or modern work inspired by them; new translations and a few established favourites are still in demand, and this book joins a whole company of writings on the ancient theatre and its authors in all degrees of specialisation.

It is worth recalling that there were centuries between the end of Antiquity and the beginnings of the modern world when the Greek theatre survived through little more than the texts of forty-odd plays by four of its authors. These were still read and copied by hand for other readers long after the last actor had taken his bow and the last theatre was abandoned to other uses or none. One can well ask how these texts are to be reconstituted as theatre, or how we can attempt to see them in any such way as the people did for whom they were written and performed; and since performances went on over a whole millennium in Antiquity, it can also be asked how production changed in style over such a long period. This book is concerned with some of the answers to those questions.

Excavation recovers theatres, and scholarship interprets their remains. Some idea can be formed of the physical dimensions of a performance, of the relationship in space between performers and audience, and also of developments in design as architects and their patrons worked to have more people see and hear better in more comfortable and impressive surroundings. Though theatres could be, and were, used for occasions other than performing plays, essentially they were buildings for special occasions, for the festivals at which plays were produced. 'Special occasions' deserves emphasis. It underlines a contrast between ancient and modern theatre to which we shall return – that a festival at which one could see a play was characteristically an event of the civil and religious calendar as well as an entertainment: there was no question of a run of performances from which one could choose (perhaps after reading a review), still less, in case it needs recalling, the option of seeing a play, or a long series of episodes in serial, in one's own home at the touch of a switch.

Playwrights wrote with the special occasion of festival production in mind. Their texts themselves sometimes show how they imagined the space would be exploited by movement and spectacle; but because they wrote in a tradition of open-air performance without special lighting or scenery, and because, in their civilisation, the spoken word had such power, the visual circumstances of a stage action could readily be created by words in the mind's eye of those who heard them. So, Sophocles' *Oedipus at Colonus* begins with the words 'Child of a blind old man, Antigone . . .'. The speaker asks where he is; he wonders who will receive him, Oedipus the wanderer; Antigone says what she can see, and in doing so tells the audience what they are to imagine. From their appearance and movements, reinforced by the words, the two actors are accepted as the blind man and his daughter; accepted also, as the blind Oedipus accepts it, is the verbal scene-painting of city walls in the distance, and nearby a grove with laurel, olive and vines, where nightingales sing, 'a sacred place, it seems'.

The relation between text as heard and spectacle as seen will recur as a topic in the chapters that follow. The visual material from the ancient world that relates to the theatre covers an enormous range in date, place of manufacture and kind. There are representations of dramatic scenes, of actors, of masks, that indispensable element of Greek theatre, on painted pottery, notably from fifth-century Athens and fourth-century Southern Italy; there are terracotta figurines, mosaics, metalware, sculpture and gems; and part of our purpose has been to give an idea of all these things in their variety and in the different reflections they give of what theatre meant to their owners. Here some further dimensions enter into the study. If we can enquire into the relationship between words and theatrical presentation, we can also enquire into the relationship between that presentation and a depiction of it in one medium or another, and at whatever remove from something actually seen. A literal-minded person might be disappointed that ancient artists and craftsmen do not work like photographers. Vivid observers though they can be, they were not at work to provide visual aids for textbooks or lectures. We can, with care, use them in that way as aids to a modern imagination, but if we do no more we risk misunderstanding them as well as losing part of the story they tell. They tell a story that ancient stills could not have done, about Greek drama as seen through the eyes of some of those who kept its classic moments and traditions alive and found a place for it in the society of their own times. In many collections all over the world where ancient art is represented there will be found objects like those that appear in this book. A visitor who responds to them or enjoys seeing them illustrated has an enhanced mental picture of the Greek theatre and its traditions which may seem akin to that given from hearing, or hearing in mind, the words of a great dramatist.

We offer here some ingredients for such a mental picture. By a rough reckoning, the British Museum has some 350 objects relating to the Greek theatre, many of them outstanding pieces in their own right. Of these, we have chosen some sixty which we think are specially interesting in one way or another, adding photographs of a few key objects from elsewhere (not forgetting theatres) to help our narrative. All of this material, including the texts referred to in presenting it, has often been (and often will be) the subject of keenly speculative discussion and argument among experts. We have often simplified what might be said, but we hope not deceptively; we hope also that fellow enthusiasts for the subject will not feel too short-changed when some of their favourites are missing, and will enjoy comparing this selection of objects with the numerous parallels to be found in other books and collections. People blame you less, according to Pindar, if you tie up the ends of numerous subjects in brief. In trying to do this, we naturally hope he is right, but we are also at work together on another, more comprehensive study.

CHAPTER 2

Song, Dance and Drama

The modern producer of an ancient Greek play finds from the first moment of looking at the cast list that, as well as a number of roles for individual actors, there is a group of people to cope with (it might, on enquiry, turn out to be twelve, fifteen or twenty-four), which will be described in the copy of the play as a chorus. From Aeschylus in the early fifth century BC to Menander in the late fourth, the part played by the chorus changes from dominance to near vanishing point. But the chorus is never totally forgotten, and Aristotle, whose general theory (detail apart) still stands, looked for the origins of tragedy and comedy in different kinds of choral performance.

A chorus, in the sense that is relevant here, means a group of people who both sing and dance. We have representations of choruses in the visual arts from times long before there are any texts to tell us what they sang. The performing chorus can be of normal-looking people; sometimes, though they are basically in human shape, they are plainly not supposed to be normal. They may be superhuman, they may represent creatures from the animal world, or they may combine elements of god, man and beast which, if thinking analytically, we moderns would try to distinguish. Perhaps a germ of drama as we know it is recognisably present when people dress up to represent someone or something other than what they are; but simple role-playing (much though we enjoy this from infancy onwards) is not enough to make drama. For Aristotle, the first principle ('or, as one might say, the soul') of tragedy was plot (*Poetics* 1450a 38f.); and so (one can similarly theorise) a well-spring of drama is opened when a chorus takes the essential step from assuming a role to enacting a role; something more happens when different parts of it respond to each other; more still happens when a leader takes a differentiated role, and the part of the actor emerges from the group. For there to be drama, by this concept, there has to be a story-line;

something has to be happening which the performers enact and do not simply narrate, even if, as we shall see, the distinction can be hard to draw.

It need hardly be stressed that this sort of reconstruction, however much one would like to make it, goes beyond any reality that can now be recovered. Performances with recognisable dramatic elements can be documented much earlier, but if we are to name a period when proto-drama became drama in the world of Greek Antiquity, that period, from many converging indications, would be in the sixth century BC, and conspicuously in its latter half.

The vase shown in fig. 1 was designed to hold wine and it was made in Corinth in the first quarter of the sixth century. The subject shown is The Return of Hephaistos. The story behind it is that the lame god Hephaistos, who was the immortals' great craftsman, once tricked his mother Hera by making a throne which imprisoned her in such a way

1 *The Return of Hephaistos, depicted in early sixth-century Corinth.*

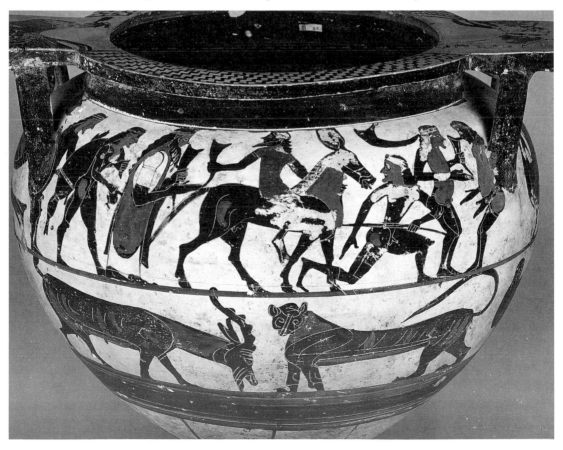

that only he could set her free. For that to happen, Dionysos had to find him, break down his resistance and bring him home happily drunk. On the vase we see Hephaistos on a mule, escorted by Dionysos and some companions, the two on the far right in the pose regularly associated with dancers, one of them holding a drinking-horn; on the far left one of the figures holds a wine-skin and jug. The subject goes on attracting vase-painters and other artists, and the scene with Dionysos, Xanthias and the donkey at the beginning of the *Frogs* of Aristophanes in 405 BC perhaps takes colour from it. Earlier in literature it is reported from a lyric narrative by Pindar and from a comedy entitled 'Revellers or Hephaestus' by one of the first generation of comic poets, Epicharmus. It is not known when these works were written, but a possible context would be in the 470s, when Hiero of Syracuse, the patron of both poets, was disabled and had to be carried into battle like the injured Philoctetes before Troy, as Pindar recalled on another occasion (*Pyth.* 1.50).

Such an image can take many forms and have many values; what interests us here, as it constantly will later, is what it was that the artist saw. The minimal assumption from the presence of the dancing figures is, perhaps, a performance of a traditional song-and-dance routine that had (or once had) a special meaning in its context, as invocation or celebration, for instance. The maximum assumption would be a re-enactment of a story in dramatic form of which the scene depicted is a key moment. We do not in any case have a context. The association of the dancers with a narrative scene is rare, but not unique; similar figures performing, so to speak, in their own right appear not only in Corinth but in several other places such as Boeotia, Sparta and East Greece; for Attica (fig. 2), though one can speak of Corinthian influence on the style, there are reasons for thinking of an independent local tradition of performance. It is acceptable that different groups of performers may have dressed and performed differently, but they are in any case depicted in different aspects by the vase-painters. They are sometimes seen as individual fertility spirits, who are given appropriate names, like 'Bender' or 'Jokey'; they can be differentiated from ordinary people by being naked, somewhat wild-looking, plump in front and behind, and sometimes grossly phallic; sometimes they dance with female companions, naked or clothed. In these aspects they are broadly analogous to the satyrs and other rampant male figures who dance with nymphs or

maenads and who are associated with later versions of the Return story. They can also be seen as performers, with the fatness as padded costume, and with the women as men dressed for the role; and in that aspect, the padded costume is recognisable as an ancestor of the comic actor's costume of the classical age and afterwards, to be illustrated and discussed later on (pp. 58ff.).

2 In Attica, an independent local tradition of dances.

The padded dancers thus represent one kind of choral performance with germs of drama in it. Of their kin the satyrs, the next chapter will say more. Figs 3 and 4 show other varieties of revel and chorus that need to be taken into account. The bird-dancers of fig. 3 are dated to the first twenty years of the fifth century. It was in 486 BC that comedy was officially recognised as an event at the Great Dionysia at Athens. A variety of play-titles and some surviving fragments of plays from that period onwards give evidence of choruses representing not only birds, but animals, insects and other creatures of the natural world; we shall see (pp. 49ff.) that Aristophanes was conscious of this tradition, and the Athenian jug of fig. 3 gives a notion of its visual character. How far performances of anything recognisable as Comedy went back beyond

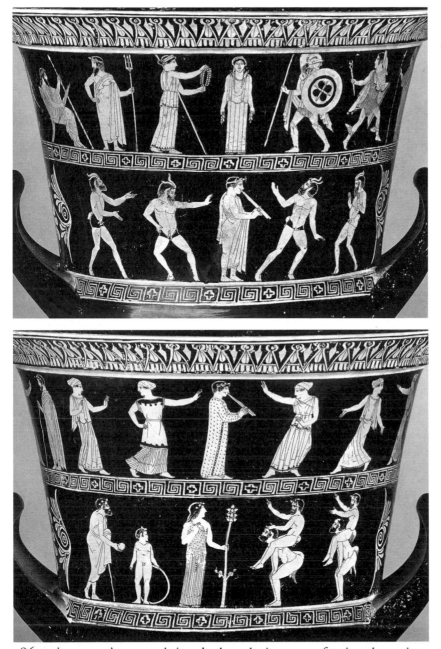

3 (*Opposite*) *A chorus of bird-dancers in early fifth-century Athens.*

4 *Choruses of Pan-dancers and of women, with other scenes.*

486 BC is anyone's guess: Aristotle thought in terms of quite a long time (*Poetics* 1449b 1f.) and there is certainly a continuous sequence of these choruses represented on vases back as far as the middle of the sixth century.

Fig. 4 has two scenes with choruses performing to pipers. One side of the vase (which is dated to 460/50 BC) has a panel with men dressed up in hairy trunks and masks with goat horns in the likeness of the god Pan; these Pan-types can be compared and contrasted with the chorus of a classical satyr-play as seen in fig. 5. Whatever their song was, it is important for us that they are a chorus in costume, shown as representing someone other than themselves: they could be a variant on a dramatic satyr-chorus, or they could be a survival of a pre- or proto-dramatic form of dance. On the other side of the vase is a representation of a chorus of women. The vase-painter has not made it obvious, at any rate to a modern eye, whether we are to see the dancing figures as women, or as a male chorus representing women; but they would be acceptable as an image of a female tragic chorus played by men just as well as one of girls singing and dancing. It is not clear how, if at all, the other two subjects are connected with these. Above the Pan-chorus, the scene in which the gods offer gifts to the newly-created Pandora, presided over by Zeus (extreme left), has a possible counterpart in drama in a lost satyr play by Sophocles entitled *Pandora*. Below the chorus of women, a family of satyrs is composed round the central figure of a maenad and includes a child with a hoop and two riding piggy-back; it is a work of the imagination to which, if one is needed, we seem to have no clue.

The possible growing points for drama in choral song are many, almost as many as the types of song we know, for elements of role-playing and narrative can be found in one way or another through the whole range from hymn of praise to lament. Remarking on the origins of Tragedy and Comedy in the *Poetics* (1449a 9–14), Aristotle thought of an evolution of chorus leader into actor in two kinds of choral performance which may have been, or may have become, especially associated with the cult of Dionysos. For Tragedy, he thought of dithyramb, which, whatever other developments it fostered, found an ecological niche to survive in its own right as a vehicle for highly-wrought lyric composition, so that the word 'dithyrambic' can be used in a derogatory way to describe airy elevation. (An idea of what dithyramb meant in Aristotle's day is given by fig. 12.) For Comedy he thought of what he describes as *ta phallika*, which he knew of as traditional in many places in Greece: old fertility rituals. Would he, one wonders, have counted the one of which Aristophanes gives a short stage sketch in the *Acharnians* (237–79)? One can guess like Aristotle, or one can guess, as some have done, on different lines from him; the miracle that escapes reconstruction is the transformation of song and dance into something that was to lead at a rapid pace to Aeschylus, Sophocles, Euripides and Aristophanes, and to their heirs and successors still with us.

CHAPTER 3

The Satyr Play

Fig. 5 is a drawing of the principal scene of a vase now in Naples datable to the end of the fifth century BC. It shows the cast of a satyr play assembled in the Sanctuary of Dionysos. Satyr play is perhaps the most difficult of the Greek dramatic genres to cope with, not least because we only learn anything about it after it has passed its prime. In essence it seems to have represented a very primitive element, built up around a chorus of men impersonating satyrs, those wild followers of Dionysos with their horses' tails and ears, snub noses and unkempt hair. The chorus was led by an Old Satyr, the *papposilenos*, who from the time of Sophocles onwards, wore all-over tights with woolly white tufts attached. There also came to be a limited number of actor roles,

normally divine or heroic. Inasmuch as we can say anything about the plays, they seem to have dealt with a restricted number of themes in which the satyr-chorus, at once timorous and aggressive, uncontrolled and biddable, took on group activities whether as sportsmen, warriors, discoverers of wine, or carers for the young. They often seem, in a 'carnevalesque' way, to have upset the status quo, the normal order of things, only to have order restored at the end of the play. Their function was one of humour and release, and by the time we come to hear much about them, they were situated within the festival as a fourth play at the end of a set of three tragedies. In 467 BC, Aeschylus' *Seven against Thebes* was produced as third to the now lost *Laios* and *Oedipus* in a trilogy on three generations of a family; this was followed by the satyr play *Sphinx*, with the monster whose power Oedipus broke by solving the riddle she set him. Such congruence was not imposed by a rule; in 438 BC, when Euripides' production included his celebrated *Telephus* (see p. 38 below), connected trilogies of tragedies were still unusual, and *Alcestis* was admitted as fourth instead of a satyr play.

Fig. 5 gives us a good idea of how a satyr play looked at the end of the fifth century. The chorusmen, here as for the other genres, are late

5 *Chorus and cast of a classical satyr play.*

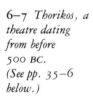

6–7 *Thorikos, a*
theatre dating
from before
500 BC.
(See pp. 35–6
below.)

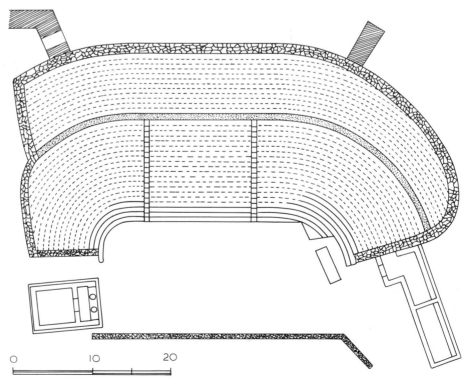

0   10   20

teenagers, and what we seem to have is a representation of the individual performers: the vase-painter has given them their names. They stand around chatting idly with their masks in their hands. It is worth noting the apparently light weight of the masks; so far as we know, they were made of stiffened linen, painted, and with hair attached as appropriate; they tended, unlike some modern imitations, to cover most of the head, and making them must have been one of the finer arts of the costume and property man, the *skeuopoios*, who had to remember, all else apart, that his masterpieces should be robust enough to stand being changed, sometimes quite rapidly, as the actors in a play took different roles. Around their hips the chorusmen, as we see, wear tights or trunks, hairy (though this was not invariably the case), with a phallos attached at the front and a horse-tail at the back. In the centre at the bottom of the scene is the chorus' piper who is named Pronomos (and the vase is therefore generally referred to as the Pronomos Vase), while the writer, Demetrios, is seen further to the left, a scroll in his hand. (It is interesting that the emphasis on the performance gives the musician, not the writer, the more prominent position.) Above, in the centre, are Dionysos as god of the theatre and his companion Ariadne. It is his sanctuary, as is also shown by the presence of tripods on columns at the sides: they were regular dedications after victories in the dramatic festivals, and the Monument of Lysikrates (fig. 12), which also had a tripod on top, is simply a more elaborate version of the same thing. To either side stand the actors from the performance, including on the upper right a Herakles.

Just to the left of centre at the bottom one of the chorusmen is dancing. He wears his mask and he is in some sense fulfilling his role. This brings us to an important issue of the principles of the depiction of drama in classical Athens. A glance at the illustrations for our section on tragedy will show that (apart from one special case to be noted) it contains no depictions of tragic actors acting, while the actors of comedy are shown in all the artificiality of their costume as actors. The reaction of the makers of the vases and figurines was that of other members of the audience. Serious theatre needs to maintain its dramatic illusion and to persuade the spectator to believe in the events unfolding on stage. The playwright and his actors were recreating the stories of the audience's own heroic history in a society which found dramatic performance

8 *Young man dancing, dressed as a satyr.*

9 *(Opposite) A cup by the Brygos Painter: satyrs in action.*

realistic and stirring. It is not surprising that when an artist represented such a performance he did so in terms of the further reality that the performers were persuading him to see; he portrayed the myth itself rather than the immediate actuality of actors on stage. Comedy, by contrast, consisted of men dressed up being funny. The comic genre in the fifth century regularly played on the interaction between audience and performer, and regularly broke the dramatic illusion by reference to itself, its practice and its costume. Just as the satyr play came between the two in its serio-comic style, so representations of it fell into the two different modes, and occasionally even combined them.

The splendid dancing figure in fig. 8 is shown as a young man dressed up as a satyr. The trunks he wears are much the same as those worn by the chorusmen on the Pronomos Vase (fig. 5), and the dance he performs seems similar to the one performed there. The date of this vase should be a little but not much earlier. On other examples such as fig. 9, however,

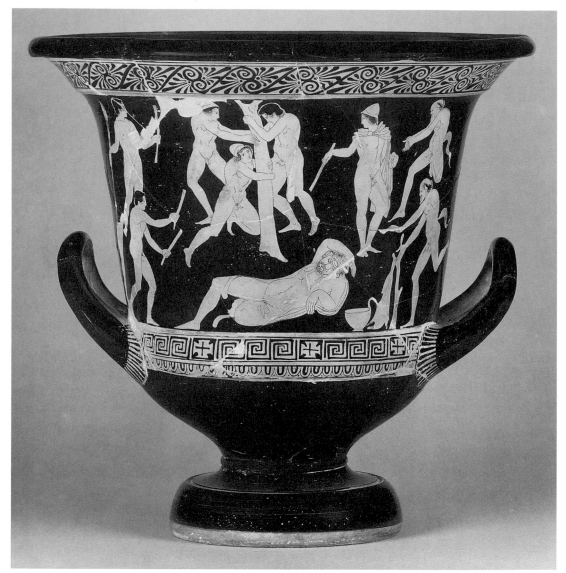

10 *Blinding the Cyclops (with satyrs suggesting a satyr play).*

the figures are shown as real satyrs. The cup shown as fig. 9 is one of the Museum's finest and it should date to the second decade of the fifth century, the period between the battles of Marathon and Salamis. On the one side we see satyrs approaching Zeus' consort Hera. She moves away in alarm while Herakles comes forward to defend her. Hermes, who perhaps brought the divinities to where the satyrs could be found, stands between. On the other side we have another scene which may have involved defence of territory. The messenger goddess Iris tries un-successfully to make off with a piece of meat, probably a tail, which had been in the course of being burned/cooked on the altar. One might suppose, too, that the altar, which stands in the middle of the scene, is in the sanctuary of Dionysos; the god moves forward, *kantharos* in hand; as a statue he had probably been standing on the podium just to the left.

Fig. 10 illustrates a fine symposium vase made in the Greek colony of Metaponto in the latter part of the fifth century, perhaps about 415–410 BC. The scene is set at night – the young men on the left carry torches. In the centre at the bottom is the figure which provides the context for the action, the Cyclops Polyphemos, with his large single eye set in the brow above the sockets for normal eyes. A bowl and a wineskin lie just by his elbow. Above, the companions of Odysseus struggle with the trunk of a tree, the burning end of which they will use to blind Polyphemos and thus make their escape. The satyrs dance up on the right, offering help. Their presence suggests that the vase-painting was probably inspired by one of our two surviving satyr plays, Euripides' *Cyclops*, produced in Athens only shortly before the date of the vase.

The satyrs on the right of the scene in fig. 10 share similar poses and are to be thought of as performing a choral dance. Their step is characteristically lively and we should think of them as moving rapidly about the orchestra, in rushes of enthusiasm and fear. By the later years of the fifth century, satyr play was no longer the major genre it had been earlier, but it continued to be produced through the fourth century and into the Hellenistic period. The satyr mask, too, remained a vital element in visual souvenirs of the theatre.

The other surviving satyr play is Sophocles' *Ichneutai*, only partly preserved on papyrus, it is true, but given a new life by its incorporation in *The Trackers of Oxyrhynchus*, by Tony Harrison, first produced at the National Theatre in London in 1991. Much later on, in another context, we refer to and illustrate the Oxyrhynchus papyrus in question, fig. 79.

CHAPTER 4

Theatre and Tragedy in
the Fifth Century

The stone which appears as fig. 11 is part of a long inscription recording prizewinners at the City Dionysia (also called Great Dionysia) in Athens. It was probably set up soon after 346 BC in or on a building whose location and purpose are uncertain; it drew on records which went back much earlier than that, and continued for some years afterwards. Records of this kind survive in different forms. Even though fragmentary, they are precious to a historian of the theatre for the dates and details they give. But beyond that, even from their sparse official language, we can learn something of the context in which plays were performed and which playwrights had in mind when they wrote them.

The festival was a state occasion. The events the inscription records were enhanced by colourful and impressive ceremonial of which we know something from other sources. In this text, each year has a formal heading with the name of the official by which the year was known: thus 'in [the year] of Philokles'; that is to say 459/8 BC – or, if we prefer, 458 BC, since we are speaking of spring (March/April), and the year's end came in summer (July/August). Proverbially, one could sail the sea safely from the time of the Dionysia, and numerous visitors could be expected, not least from satellites of the imperial city bringing their revenue as tribute. For the winter festival, the Lenaia (January/February), there was a sense, which Aristophanes could exploit when it suited him, that the resident population was on its own and that the behaviour of politicians was a matter of public concern wholly appropriate in a topical play (A. *Ach.* 502–8).

Under the dateline, each year has entries for the winners of boys' choir, men's choir, performers of comedy and performers of tragedy; for

col.i   col.ii   col.iii

9

12

15

18

11 *Prize-winners at the City Dionysia.*

9   [ʼΕπὶ Φιλο]κλέου[ς
     [Οἰν]ηὶς παίδων
     Δημόδοκος ἐχορήγει
12   ʽΙπποθωντὶς ἀνδρῶν
     Εὐκτήμων ʼΕλευ:(σίνιος) ἐχορή(γει)
     κωμωιδῶν
15   Εὐρυκλείδης ἐχορήγει
     Εὐφρόνιος ἐδίδασκε
     τραγωιδῶν
18   Ξενοκλῆς ʼΑφιδνα:(ῖος) ἐχορή(γει)
     ┌─────────────────────────┐
     │ Αἰσχύλος ἐδίδασκεν   │
     └─────────────────────────┘

12 *Dionysos and the pirates: the monument of Lysikrates, 334* BC.

each of these a sponsor (*choregos*) is named, the individual who undertook to support the occasion as a public service from his private funds. For the choral events, choirs of fifty performed compositions under the traditional name of dithyramb; the performers came from the ten tribes which comprised the Athenian citizen community, and the successful tribe is named. If all ten tribes took part with men and boys, there were 1000 performers in all; three tragic productions with choruses of twelve (or, later, fifteen) and five comic plays with twenty-four each must have added significantly to the demand, even if there was some overlapping. There must have been a strong sense of community interest and involvement, and it may be a sign of decline when in the late fourth or early third century Menander has a character in a play speak of choruses made up to number with a few tail-enders who do not sing (*Epikleros* frg. 153). Fig. 12 illustrates a monument, still in place in Athens, which was put up by the *choregos* Lysikrates to celebrate a victory with the boys' choir of the tribe Akamantis in the year we call 334 BC. The bronze tripod dedicated in honour of the victory originally stood on top, more tripods in relief sculpture make a decoration between the columns, and the frieze above depicts the critical action in an adventure of Dionysos which presumably figured in the winning performance. The story, known from the Homeric *Hymn to Dionysos* and elsewhere, is of the capture of Dionysos by pirates: here his satyr companions fight with their captors, some of whom are seen being transformed by the god into dolphins.

We return to fig. 11. For the performers of comedy and tragedy (and note that chorus and actors are here treated as a group), the inscription names the playwright, but – interestingly – with the traditional formula *edidasken* ('was the producer') which assumes that the individual who wrote the lines also taught the chorus and actors how to perform them. Occasions are recorded in which playwrights took an actor's part themselves, and they may often have done so in the earliest days; the fact that the word used for producing a play is the same as that used for teaching young people in school reminds us that, in theory at any rate, the playwright is not simply the person responsible for the text, but the person responsible for the performance, someone we would call the director. There are known occasions when a first performance at a festival was produced by someone other than the playwright (this happened several times in the career of Aristophanes, for instance); what rules governed the practice we do not know.

Of the people commemorated for success in the Dionysia of 458 BC, little or nothing is known, until we come to the last line for the year, when the words 'Aeschylus was the producer' record the first production of the *Oresteia*.

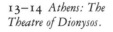

13–14 *Athens: The Theatre of Dionysos.*

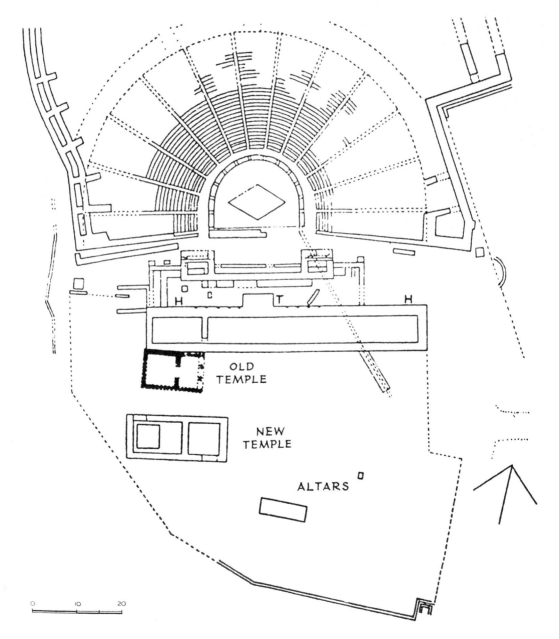

OLD TEMPLE

NEW TEMPLE

ALTARS

0   10   20

The first production of the *Oresteia* was seen by perhaps ten thousand people in the Theatre of Dionysos, figs 13–14. It is hard to be precise about the size of the fifth-century auditorium, but for our purposes we hardly need be. The essential point is that the audience was more like a moderate-sized football crowd than a modern indoor theatre-full. The surviving ruins, though much overlaid by later epochs of construction, give a visitor some sense of scale and sight-lines. It is still debated at what date Wall H, the long line of conglomerate blocks with their rectangular platform and slots for beams, was laid down to make a base for the stage-building. If that was not until the fourth century, we cannot depend on having any securely identifiable remains of the theatre of classical tragedy and fifth-century comedy.

The stage at this period has to be thought of as a low platform, possibly as much as 20 metres long, connected by a low step or steps with an orchestra of matching dimensions. The orchestra is the domain of the chorus, physically as well as intellectually and emotionally intermediate between actors and audience. How early it took its familiar circular form, as at Epidauros (figs 32–33) is undetermined; for the fifth century we have perhaps to think of the Theatre of Dionysos as a metropolitan version of Thorikos (figs 6–7) or Trachones, with auditorium and orchestra rectilinear rather than circular, but with an orchestra at any rate big enough to accommodate with ease such spectacles as the round dance by a chorus of 24 in Aristophanes' *Thesmophoriazusae* (953ff.) in 411 BC. Actors enter from either side, or from the stage building. The opening lines of *Agamemnon*, the first play of the *Oresteia*, are spoken by a guard who presents himself as being on the roof of the royal place. By 458 BC, then, if not earlier, the building is solid enough to have a practicable roof and to give an acceptable impression of a palace. A palace is the regular setting for classical tragedy, with its stories of disaster to royal families; dire events may happen within it, and be told abroad outside; it is a hinge of the play when Agamemnon descends from his chariot and walks on the precious purple cloth, as if on blood, to the dark inside where Clytemnestra will murder him. In tragedy only a single central door is used and attention focuses on it all the more when that is needed. The decor is likely to have been formal and conventional: the scenery is created by words in the mind's eye; the words, by turns bolder, more colourful, and more precise than in real life (in comedy both neater at times and more outrageous) will have required a larger-than-life style of acting to deliver them. Tourists are sometimes surprised by the fine acoustics of ancient theatres; but on seeing performances in them, one is left in no doubt of the excellence of excellent actors and the merits and demerits of the ordinary. An important element in the development of Greek drama is the growth of the actors' role vis à vis that of the chorus, and one can see one factor in this in the physical conditions of production.

Fig. 24 (see frontis. and p. 47 below) shows a fourth-century artist's impression from *Eumenides*, the third play of the *Oresteia*, with Orestes taking refuge at Delphi, in a tableau with Apollo, Athena and Furies. When in Aristophanes' *Frogs* (1124) the opening speech of the second play, *Choephoroe*, is quoted as 'the prologue from the *Oresteia*', the implication may well be that before the end of the fifth century *Choephoroe* and *Eumenides*, produced together, had already begun a repertory life of their own. The Euripidean *Orestes* certainly became a famous repertory play, and it is commemorated in a wall-painting of Roman Imperial date to be considered later (fig. 71).

Scenes of supplication or refuge at an altar provide memorable

incidents for tragedy because they present in clear visual form, and with an appeal to religious feelings, a knot or crisis in the action. Such scenes, let it be said, were by no means the only way that dramatists found to

15 *Telephos on the altar with Orestes.*

exploit the essentially static nature of the staging of classical tragedy: to recall *Frogs* again, Aeschylus was evidently well remembered for the long statuesque silence of his mourning Niobe in her name play, or of his Achilles in the *Myrmidons* (*Frogs* 911ff.). Fig. 15 shows a more aggressive suppliant than Orestes, who in fact appears in this scene as an infant; Telephos, the exiled ruler of Mysia, at the palace of Agamemnon, seized Orestes, the king's son, and held him with him on the altar. This vase, dated to the mid-fifth century, is too early to reflect the famous treatment of the episode in Euripides' play *Telephus* of 438 BC, in which Telephos threatened the child's life with a sword. It has therefore been associated with Aeschylus, who died in Sicily in 456 BC, and might well have been in mind when it was painted. It was the Euripidean version of Telephos and the baby that inspired Aristophanes' parodies in *Acharnians* and *Thesmophoriazusae*; a look ahead to fig. 27 and pp. 52–3 documents this and offers a good chance to contrast the tragic mode with the comic. Oineus, king of Calydon, is mentioned in *Acharnians* (418ff.) along with Telephos and others as one of Euripides' pathetic heroes in distress. Fig. 25 has been associated with the play, and shows him as an old man being brought forward to have his revenge, with the help of Diomedes, on his usurping brother Agrios. Oineus, now restored, is robed as a tragic king; Agrios, whose identity is provided by the vase-painter, is bound like a prisoner, apparently awaiting sacrifice on an altar. By the altar, as a symbol of vengeance, is a black Fury brandishing a snake.

The sufferings of the heroes of tragedy can be literally spectacular and were surely designed to be so: there are recognisable exceptions to the general rule that tragedy does not bring violence and suffering on stage. An obvious example is Prometheus, who is seen being chained to a cliff at the beginning of *Prometheus Bound*; there is also Ixion, tortured on the wheel for an attempted sexual assault on Hera. This is a motif we met in fig. 9: it is known in connection with Ixion from plays now lost, and fig. 16 is thought to reflect the Aeschylean version.

An innovation of the fifth-century theatre was a device like a platform on wheels, called *ekkyklema*, which could be rolled out from the central door to display interior scenes. Like the crane which could deliver gods from Heaven, or allow characters to fly up to it (as Bellerophon did on his magic horse Pegasos in Euripides), this mechanical device may not have

16 *Ixion condemned to the wheel.*

appealed to everyone's imagination, and it certainly gave writers of comedy some fine chances for a send-up. But the technique of interior display is used seriously in Sophocles' *Ajax* to show Ajax surrounded by the carcasses of the animals he has slaughtered in the belief that they are the Greek leaders who slighted him; in *Prometheus Bound*, by contrast, the platform could have been rolled out at the beginning of the play and used to withdraw the hero, still chained, at the end. It could have been used similarly in plays about Ixion, if his torture was to be shown and not narrated.

A very striking stage spectacle was the binding of Andromeda, whose mother's boast of being more beautiful than the sea-nymphs caused Poseidon to send a monster; her father Kepheus had then to face the situation of offering Andromeda to it as a sacrifice. A group of vases dating from 450/440 BC, of which fig. 17 illustrates one, are thought to

17 *Andromeda made ready for the monster.*

reflect enthusiasm for the production of an *Andromeda* by Sophocles. Here we see the grim preparations for tying her to the stakes, as servants bring her to the scene; others carry offerings, as for the dead; Kepheus supervises; further round the vase Perseus, who will rescue her, looks on as from a distance. There is some evidence that Aeschylus' son Euaion acted in the play and took the role of Perseus. Euripides' version was produced in 412 BC; its beginning is known in part from Aristophanes' topical parody in the *Thesmophoriazusae* (1056ff.), which was produced in the following year. It was different in having Andromeda discovered at the start already secured to a rock (not unlike Prometheus) and lamenting in the dark with the nymph Echo for company. This version can be distinguished in vase-paintings from the Sophoclean one, even if there is some contamination between them in later representations.

Another suffering hero, Phineus, appears in fig. 18, shown with blind eyes, and with his food being stolen by Harpies; the vase-painter gives

him the words 'O gods, gods'. Aeschylus produced a *Phineus* in the same production as his *Persae* of 472 BC, and a special mask for the blind Phineus is listed in the catalogue of dramatic masks compiled by Pollux for his *Onomasticon* (4.141); Pollux dedicated this encyclopedia to the Emperor Commodus (AD 180–193), but the vase must be close to the date of the play.

18 *Phineus blinded: 'O gods, gods . . .'*

Violence on the tragic stage, like suffering, can be brought home to audiences by narrative as well as symbolic enactment; and when incidents from plays now lost are depicted in art, it is not always clear how much translation from words to vision is involved. In Euripides' *Hercules Furens*, Iris, as messenger from Hera, brings Lyssa, daughter of Night, to drive the hero mad; an impassioned lyric intervention by the chorus is cut through by cries from within the house, raising the emotional temperature for a long narrative (922–1015) of the storm of delusion in which Herakles murders the very children he has just rescued

from death. A similar dramatic sequence could have been the basis for the Madness of Lycurgus, as depicted in fig. 19, by a vase-painter working in Taranto shortly before the middle of the fourth century, which is described with some of its contemporaries in Chapter 6, pp. 69–70. What concerns us here is that the likely source for this image is a lost play of Aeschylus first produced in Athens a good hundred years earlier, namely *Edonoi*, the first play of the trilogy *Lykourgeia*, which we can guess was already established as a classic in later fifth-century Athens from Aristophanes' reference to it in *Thesmophoriazusae* and from motifs which seem to have been picked up from Aeschylus by Euripides in the *Bacchae*. It is fascinating that the theme suddenly reappears in contemporary art also.

19 *The Madness of Lycurgus.*

20 *Sophocles'* Oedipus Tyrannus: *fateful news from Corinth.*

Narrative plays a different and interestingly contrasting role in four more representations with which this chapter concludes; all will be looked at again in another context in Chapter 6. Fig. 20 represents Sophocles' *Oedipus Tyrannus* as seen in terms of a stage performance by a fourth-century vase-painter. The moment in the plot which is recalled is one which was especially commended for its tragic quality by Aristotle in the *Poetics* (1452a 22ff.). The messenger, seen on the left, thinks he has news which will relieve Oedipus' anxieties; in fact that news reveals to Jocasta, who has already begun to recognise the truth, and then to Oedipus himself, that Oedipus has after all met his foretold fate of killing his father, all unknown, and marrying his mother. The audience, with superior knowledge, anticipates the full horror which will uncoil on the characters as the scene develops (924ff.).

Fig. 21 is a typically elaborate fourth-century presentation of a theme from Euripides' *Hippolytus*, the young hero's fatal chariot-ride into exile, which the messenger, again seen on the left, will narrate (1153ff.). The

21 *The Death of Hippolytus.*

22 *Sacrifice and transformation of Iphigeneia.*

owner of the vase no doubt recalled the speech: the bull, sent by Poseidon in response to Theseus' curse on his son, rises from the sea; the panic that struck the horses is personified by a Fury; a composition of gods, some closely connected with the play, some no more than marginally, presides over the scene from the upper register.

Not unlike this in some ways is fig. 22, which surely reflects Euripides' *Iphigeneia at Aulis*. Here again we see the shock of an event which occurs off-stage. The whole action has led up to the moment when Agamemnon sacrifices his daughter to gain a fair wind for sailing to Troy, and at that moment she is transformed into a deer. The trans-

23 *Euripides'* Phoenissae: *Antigone goes to watch the Seven advance on Thebes.*

24 *Orestes takes refuge at Delphi.*

25 *King Oineus restored: revenge at last.*

formation brings a resolution of a crisis and the beginning of a new life for Iphigeneia. It was a memorable happy ending, even if the text of the play has suffered 'improvements' on whatever it was that Euripides originally planned.

The picturesque and romantic side of Greek tragedy, especially late Euripides, has been glimpsed, no more, in our mention above of his treatment of Andromeda. Fig. 23 may do a little to redress the balance. It shows the young Antigone being escorted to the palace roof in Thebes by an elderly servant, who will show her, excited as she is by a mixture of fright and curiosity, the advancing seven champions from Argos and their forces. Euripides' reworking in *Phoenissae* (88–201) of the scene from *Iliad* 3 (161–244) with Priam and Helen on the walls of Troy, has a blend of qualities, literary, operatic and spectacular, which evidently created a memorable image.

CHAPTER 5

Aristophanes and Others: The Comedy of Classical Athens

For classical tragedy, we have plays by three major dramatists ranging in date from 472 BC to near the end of the century. For comedy, until Menander in the last quarter of the fourth century, most of what can be known depends on the surviving selection of plays by a single author, Aristophanes. The selection favours the political and satirical comedies of Aristophanes' earlier years, with five plays dating from 425 to 421 BC; it then has six more at intervals in the remaining thirty-five years or so of his active career, concluding with the *Plutus* of 388, when he had moved conspicuously towards the plainer and more socially oriented style of comedy which was to come to the fore in the fourth century. There are ways in which this picture of Aristophanes can be complemented and qualified, but it still dominates.

The fact that popular entertainment is often topical and a mirror of the contemporary world should not obscure the consideration that it also often relies on good old routines and familiar traditions, which audiences enjoy because they feel at home with them. Aristophanes is no exception. The plays with choruses that represent wasps, or birds, or frogs look back quite consciously to a long tradition of song and dance by performers representing creatures of the wild or semi-feral beings like those presented above in Chapter 2. In the *Knights* (519ff.), Aristophanes mentions his predecessor Magnes, who won a first at the festivals as early as 472 BC, and had choruses of lyre-players, flapping birds, Lydians, gall-flies and frogs all-in-green. Accordingly, for Aristophanes' own play *Birds*, it is reasonable to refer back to fig. 3, which is of Magnes' generation, even if it does not represent the play by

26 An aquatic adventure: a man rowing a fish.

Magnes that we know of (as a title *Ornithes* could as well refer to cockerels as to birds in general).

Fig. 26, the man rowing a fish, gives a triple perspective. He could be a member of a chorus, even though he is a single figure and without a piper, unlike the cockerels of fig. 3. Among the vases like fig. 3 which depict pre-dramatic or proto-dramatic choruses, there are representations of men riding dolphins, strange-looking soldiers on horseback (distant ancestors of the chorus of Aristophanes' *Knights*), and, from the avian world, men riding ostriches. The fish-rower seems to belong in this tradition. Very like our vase, so much so that we seem to be dealing with a set of wine jugs made for a party to celebrate a particular production, are some fragments from a well in Athens in a context of *c*. 415–410 BC. It has been suggested that they illustrate the *Taxiarchoi* ('The Captains at Sea') by Aristophanes' contemporary Eupolis, in which, among other exciting events, Sophocles was parodied and Dionysos was given a rowing lesson by the famous Athenian naval commander Phormion, who may have been brought back from the dead to do that: 'Stop splashing us, that man in the bows', reads a snatch of words recovered from a papyrus. Much of this is conjectural, but the rowing lesson at least is certain, and if it recalls Dionysos being taught to row by Charon in the *Frogs* (197ff.), one should not be surprised. Rumours flew around in Antiquity, and ring in scholars' ears today, about collaboration, imitation, even sheer plagiarism between the two rival playwrights; with a rich fund of common material available, the line must sometimes have been hard to draw.

Among comic characters with a long history (and a long future to come) is Herakles (fig. 34). His gargantuan appetite, among other qualities, made him a natural (if somewhat awesome) figure of fun for comedy, and so he appears in a fragment of one of the earliest comic writers, the Sicilian Epicharmus, snorting, grinding and gulping through his meal in a way fit to frighten you to death. Aristophanes in the *Wasps* writes of 'Herakles cheated of his dinner' as something thoroughly old hat (60); but (not at all untypically of him) makes use of the Herakles-and-food routine when it suits him to do so in *Frogs* (549–78). The group of early terracottas to which the Herakles belongs can be quoted to document comic costume in Aristophanes' later years, at the end of the fifth century and in the early fourth; and some other characters

27 *Telephos on the altar: a parody by Aristophanes.*

in it, like the Herakles, may go back considerably further. Plays quite often begin with people going somewhere (*Birds*, for instance) or have travellers arriving, as at the beginning of *Plutus*, and fig. 35 is an illustration in point. That traveller brings the story away from the realm of myth and fantasy into the everyday world, but for fifth-century comedy that world is interpenetrated by myth and fantasy, and before we leave them two more vases must be quoted. Fig. 27 is one of the more exciting accessions to knowledge of recent years. Careful study of the detail links the scene inescapably with the parody of Euripides' *Telephus* in Aristophanes' *Thesmophoriazusae* (689–759); for instance, the wine-skin which replaces baby Telephos has the bootees referred to in the play (733f.); and, as in the play, there is a woman with a bowl to catch the blood (that is, the wine) from the sacrifice. It is a stock joke that women never miss the chance of a drink; what is not given by the text but does appear in the representation, is that the woman, who is addressed by the pet-name Mikka ('Little-one', 760), is seen to be remarkably ugly as her cloak suddenly falls from her face.

A notable feature of the development of Greek comedy is that motifs and structures which are first introduced by way of parody and burlesque of tragedy somehow take root in their new environment and continue as part of the comic tradition; the idiom of mythological comedy no doubt helps this to happen. The scenes of refuge at an altar, like fig. 15, have their comic counterpart not only in parody, as here, but in 'real-life' scenes such as those with miscreant slaves, who, like the man in the *Thesmophoriazusae* scene, may be threatened with being burnt out by a bonfire. An example from later comedy is a scene of Menander's *Perinthia*, of which part survives in a papyrus fragment, and there are numerous terracotta models of figures on altars, both earlier and later than Menander: see fig. 41 and pp. 65–7 below.

The Telephos vase was painted in Taranto about 380–370 BC, some thirty years after the first production of *Thesmophoriazusae*. There is no way to tell if it recorded the first or a later performance of the play there; but we should recall that the South Italian vase reflecting Euripides' satyr play *Cyclops* (fig. 10) was painted at a date close to that of the original Athenian production. It has long been argued that many of the comic scenes on South Italian vases represent productions of Athenian comedies. What is interesting is the growing amount of evidence that some of these plays were not contemporary or recent Athenian comedies, but classic revivals. One wonders about a play such as that found in fig. 28. The figure of Cheiron the centaur recalls the title *Cheirones* ('Cheiron and Company', referring to the chorus) by Aristophanes' much older contemporary Cratinus, as well as plays entitled *Cheiron* by Pherecrates in the fifth century and Cratinus the Younger in the fourth, but it is hard to say whether the vase represents a mythological comedy in fifth-century style or in the style which we know of from titles and fragments as very popular later. These scenes and others like them, whether from contemporary plays or revivals, reflect the practices and conventions which were familiar to their buyers, and there will be more to say of them in Chapter 6. But the more convincingly we can identify elements in them that are traditional, the more they help to build up our image of the theatre of Aristophanes.

In Aristophanes' *Wasps*, there is an interesting example of role-reversal, in which a son escorts his drunken father, plus temporary girl

28 Uphill work: Chiron the centaur in a comedy now lost.

friend, from what should have been, but was not, an elegant symposium: 'If you're not a naughty girl now, Pussy, I'll set you free and keep you as my mistress when my son's dead . . . you see, I'm his only father' (1351ff.). It can be argued from this wrong-way-round joke, as well as from other evidence, that the kind of play which featured young men in riotous partying and love-affairs and the conflicts within families that spring from these – the basic stuff of comedy in the age of Menander

— was in fact more fully developed in the fifth century than the amount of surviving evidence would lead one to suppose: how far, after all, is it likely to be a fair sample? Be that as it may, on the basis of the *Wasps* scene, there is at least some justification for referring here to fig. 29, with the old man dragging his slave companion along to (or from) a party instead of being escorted by him. Likewise, to make the point that

29 *'Do come along': a man drags a slave by the wrist.*

30 *'Please listen': a man calls at a girl's door.*

Aristophanes' fourth-century comedies look both forward and back, we can recall the scene in *Ecclesiazusae* where the lover serenades the girl at her window (961ff. 'Run down and open the door, or I'll drop down dead'); and we can put it alongside vases which most naturally link with plays of a later period: examples are fig. 30, in which a man calls at a woman's door, and fig. 31, the lover and a companion taking a ladder to climb up to a woman at a window. The last has another version by the same artist, in which the two men are characterised as Zeus and Hermes; it carries us into the style of mythological comedy which Plautus preserved, and was to propagate in later ages, from the Greek play he adapted as *Amphitruo*.

31 *Storming party: the lover with the ladder.*

CHAPTER 6

The Theatre in the Fourth Century

Aristophanes' *Frogs*, produced in 405 BC, was taken in Antiquity and generally still is taken to mark the end of an era. Euripides and Sophocles had died the year before and Aristophanes would apparently have us believe that there were no tragic playwrights left who were worth listening to. In fact no play by any later tragedian survives. Again, until recent times, we had no comedies by anyone after Aristophanes. One might wonder if the Greek theatre lost all powers of invention with the end of the fifth century. Even the recurring images of its great dramatists as grave old men, like the fine Sophocles of fig. 78, seem to give an air of things past. Yet the more we look at the archaeological evidence, the clearer it seems that theatre gained rather than lost in popularity.

Not only did the Theatre of Dionysos at Athens (figs 13–14) have a major reconstruction under Lycurgus in the 330s, but sites such as Epidauros (figs 32–33), not one of Greece's major centres, had huge theatres built at much the same period. It has been argued that the very form of these theatres, with circular orchestra backed by high-reaching stone seating, was designed to improve acoustics for large audiences on the theory that sound spread in a circular motion. Whatever the case, these elaborate and expensive theatres reflect the growing impact of the plays performed in them both geographically and, it seems, on a broader cross-section of society.

One body of archaeological material demonstrates a number of developments that were already under way by the end of the fifth century, namely a series of terracotta figurines from Comedy, of which figs 34–37 are examples. They are standard types with standardised masks. The characters are recognisable from one example to another as

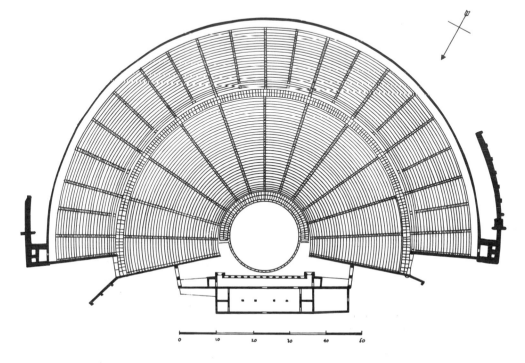

32–3 *Epidauros: the theatre, later fourth century BC.*

34 *Herakles, a traditional figure of Comedy.*

35 *The traveller on his way.*

slave, old man or nurse, and they must have been so the moment they came on stage. They argue, therefore, for a new style of comedy which is based on an interplay of stock characters, a kind of situation comedy. Moreover, the figurines were also produced as part of a standard limited series and not as reflecting any particular play. Thus the popular figure of Herakles, legs crossed, leaning on his club and with his bow in his left hand (fig. 34) is found over a long period and must have been conceived as a typical Herakles, not as one belonging to a particular situation. Similarly the traveller, fig. 35, who wears the *pilos* or traveller's cap and a cloak about his shoulders is a type who would fit many plays; the right hand on hip gives him a slightly aggressive attitude, but it is not enough to make him particular. The others, like the old nurse carrying a baby (fig. 36), or the young woman pulling up her cloak in front of her face as if to hide (fig. 37), all display a certain movement or style which emphasises or brings out their character, and it is a strong element in making them attractive. We should imagine them painted in bright colours, of which nowadays only occasional traces remain.

The figurines of this series were produced over as much as fifty years (fig. 37 is known in at least sixteen replicas, not to mention several variants) and they must have been thought relevant to comedy throughout this period. They demonstrate to us the characters popular with the audiences who bought them as souvenirs. We should also reflect that although they were originally conceived and manufactured in Athens, these figurines were exported all over the Greek world and even widely copied. Fig. 36 is said to be from Athens, fig. 35 from Tanagra in Boeotia, fig. 34 from the island of Melos. Others from the same series have been found, both originals and copies, at mainland sites such as Delphi and Corinth; on other islands including Crete and Rhodes, or up north in Thasos, and at Olynthos; at sites in Asia Minor, South Russia, and North Africa; in South Italy at Taranto and Paestum; in Sicily, notably at Syracuse; in Lipari, and at Ampurias in Spain. This distribution demonstrates the wide and rapid spread in the popularity of Athenian comedy in the early fourth century. It also reinforces the impression given by the fragmentary literary evidence, that Athenian comedy was becoming more universal in its appeal, less concerned with the here and now and more with human behaviour in general.

It may be that contemporaries saw this kind of theatre as more naturalistic than that of the previous generation. This is always a comparative process. To our eyes the costume of the actors appears crude and rather primitive, and apart from the masks, it seems to have changed little from Old Comedy in the later fifth century. The actors were still all male. They wore padding on the belly and rump in a tradition that went back to the padded dancers of the seventh and sixth centuries (figs 1–2). Over that they wore all-over tights which ended at ankle and wrist, as can be seen clearly on figurines such as the Herakles, fig. 34, or the traveller, fig. 35. The tights are clearer still in vase-paintings, such as figs 28 and 30, and many show the seams down the sides of the legs and arms, as in fig. 29, and in added colour in fig. 31. Onto the tights was attached a large phallos which we know from literary sources was of leather. On the figurines and vase-paintings it is sometimes shown as tied up (as on the Herakles, fig. 34), sometimes hanging loose (fig. 28). This much of the costume served as the actor's 'dramatic skin'. Over it he wore the clothes appropriate to the part, whether the mask and clothing of an old nurse or a girl, as in figs 36 and 37, which conceals the phallos (they are not pregnant but simply have the standard padding under-neath), or the short jerkin of the males which leaves the phallos exposed. The males sometimes wear a cloak or a mantle, and Herakles has his lion-skin. Whatever the case on stage, the figures as depicted often carry identifying attributes, such as baggage for travellers, club and bow for Herakles, baby for nurse, basket or kitchen equipment for cook, and so on.

36 *A nurse with a baby.*

For technical reasons the vases can come closer to the actual stage performance, even though, except for pieces like figs 31 and 42, their colour-range tends to be limited. As we have seen, there was a long tradition in Athens of vases showing comic performances. The Birds vase (fig. 3) is an example; it also reminds us of the way that vases refer to a particular performance rather than to a character or type, as with the terracotta figurines. This tradition continued sporadically on Athenian vases – another example is fig. 26. From the end of the fifth century, however, the idea was picked up by vase-painters in other centres such as Corinth and Elis, or Taranto, Paestum and Capua. The idea was to prove popular, and the vases of Taranto and Paestum in particular provide us with a full and lively series. The identity of costume and mask with those found on Athenian terracottas, the occasional inscription in Attic dialect

37 *A young woman hiding her face.*

rather than the locally-used Doric, and then the odd identifiable Athenian play (such as fig. 27) show that the plays were often imported Athenian. A passage in Plato's *Laws* (659A–D) written near the middle of the fourth century confirms the popularity and importance of theatre in South Italy and Sicily. Comedy, indeed all theatre, was becoming international, even if Athens remained its metropolis and attracted the

38 *A locally-made terracotta from Corinth,* 400/350 BC.

major playwrights. This is not to say that there could not be local drama, whether in South Italy (the comic poet Alexis is said to have come from Thurii and presumably learned the rudiments of his trade locally) or indeed in Corinth. Fig. 38 is an excellent example. It is made of Corinthian clay and is of typically Corinthian style. The head was made in a mould and has a mask that is recognisable in Athenian terms. The body, unlike the Athenian, is hand made and has the typical flaring skirt to the chiton that is characteristic of Corinthian figurines of this period.

The vases also show us something of the conditions of theatre production. Thus fig. 28 illustrates the steps normally found at the centre of the stage. They are wooden and lead up to a low wooden stage which from this and other evidence seems to have been about a metre high. Whatever the material of the stage-building, most stages seem to have been of wood (and for the floor of the stage wood is still preferred even nowadays). The front of the stage in the earlier half of the fourth century often seems to have been supported by posts as we see in fig. 28, but the Paestan vase (fig. 29) of the third quarter of the century shows them elaborated into columns. Figs 28 and 30 give some idea of the door, which has a small porch with projecting roof, simple on fig. 28 (but note the decorated roof), more elaborate with side column and carved swan-head support on fig. 30. To the side of the door was a window such as we see on fig. 31. This vase dates to the mid-fourth century; but we have evidence from Aristophanes, whether from *Wasps* (379) or from *Ecclesiazusae* (see above p. 56), that it was present already in his day. Two other aspects are noticeable. One is the lack of anything that could be regarded as scenery. This is important, for it tells us a great deal about the nature of ancient theatre and the way that it created its own world in the imagination of the audience. The other is that, just as on the Shakespearean stage, the props are portable and were generally carried on and off in the course of the action. Again Aristophanes helps, with the portable altar that figures in *Peace* (938).

The vase-painters represented particular plays and made them for people who had seen the plays. They therefore had no problems with the identification and we never find the name of the play given. These unidentified scenes remind us how much we have lost, and pieces such as the scene from Aristophanes' *Thesmophoriazusae* (fig. 27) are very much the exception. On fig. 28 we have three labels for individual figures,

'Chiron' for the old man with stick being heaved up the stairs, 'Xanthias' for the figure at the top dragging him up, and 'Nymphs' for the two ugly old women talking to each other in the top right-hand corner. Xanthias is a common slave-name; we can see from the mask with its bald head and thick side-hair that he played the part of a cook. The same mask occurs on fig. 42. Already on the stage is the travel-pack with which the two white-haired figures arrived: the big fat bed-roll, the yoke for carrying it across the shoulder, and a bucket-like vessel called a *situla*, normally used for carrying wine. We see another version of the same vessel on fig. 29.

Fig. 30 shows another use of the stage facilities. Here a male figure tries to encourage a girl to come out of the house. Her hesitation, signified by the use of the cloak, reminds us of the terracotta figurine, fig. 37. The figures have sometimes been described as lovers at a door, but the male could be a slave involved in an intrigue on behalf of his master, a situation which becomes very popular in New Comedy in the later part of the century. The theme seen in fig. 31, one of the Museum's better-known vases, is found in several versions. It is evening (note the torch), after a party (note the wine-situla, the festive sash, the wreaths about the men's heads and in the hand of the one on the right). The wine gives the men inspiration and courage to make their secret approach. All these scenes give some sense of the bustle and energy of Greek comic performance, and so too on fig. 29 where the master with white hair, long white beard, fancy cloak and staff has problems making his slave come along with him to (or possibly from) a party. The goose is probably elaboration on the part of the vase-painter, who may be trying to tell us that it is already morning.

The vases show us particular scenes; with the help of the terracottas, we can start to discern the popular characters and situations and see how they change through time. In the comedy of the earlier fourth century, the stage is dominated by males. Mythological burlesque with characters such as Herakles (or indeed Cheiron) is also popular. We find disputes between master and slave and complaints from the slave about what he has to put up with, especially the carrying of heavy baggage or being beaten (both of them themes present in Aristophanes' *Frogs*). By the middle and third quarter of the fourth century the women are given a more important role, like the more forward and attractive *hetairai*

(courtesans) of figs 39 and 40 with their elaborate hairstyles. They may not have had many lines on stage, but they become more and more the focus of attention and figurines of them are therefore popular items for purchase. We are moving towards the intricate intrigue comedies typical of New Comedy. This is also the context for the slave seated on an

39–40 Hetairai, *professional girlfriends, with elaborate hairstyles, 350/325 BC.*

altar (fig. 41). He takes refuge because he has been up to mischief, even if that mischief has been for good ends and he has been misunderstood. This figure is a precursor of many others of whom we shall see examples (figs 53, 54, 55 and 66). We may note too that the costume slowly changes. The phallos, for example, becomes steadily less prominent:

41 *A slave takes refuge on an altar, 330/310 BC.*

compare fig. 34 or fig. 28 with fig. 29 and then with figs 41 and 42. With hindsight we can see this as a move towards greater naturalism; for the women, figs 39 and 40, there is hardly any noticeable padding on the belly even if it survives for the slaves, in a convention which lasts as long as ancient comedy itself.

Fig. 42 is a fine depiction of a cook of very soon after the middle of the fourth century. The setting is a sanctuary: note the *boukrania* (ox-skulls) hanging in the background. The cook brings out the material for a feast. This is a scene often associated with the end of a comedy, but it is also appropriate for the use of the vessel on which the scene is placed, a symposium vase for wine. This is an aspect of comedy to which we shall return. Compare the mask of an old man from comedy hanging amid vines on another Tarentine symposium vase of the same date (fig. 43).

Examining tragedy in this period is not easy; but we can make some deductions about its character and the basis of its undoubted popularity. No plays written during the period survive, although there was a huge output and some of the tragedians acquired great stature. The younger

42 *Wine-bowl for a party: the caterer sets out a table.*

ΔΙΟΣ ΣΩΤΗΡ

43 Wine bowl for a party, with comic mask and decorative vine surround.

Carcinus (whose grandfather was also a tragic poet and whose father Xenocles had defeated Euripides in 415 BC) wrote some 160 plays, Astydamas (who counted Aeschylus amongst his ancestors) wrote 240, and Theodectes (who died at the age of forty-one) some 50. 'Classic' plays, primarily by Euripides, became a regular feature of the City Dionysia from 386 BC. They too became popular and served frequently as reference points for quotation in contemporary society. Actors became increasingly important figures, the most admired of them commanding huge fees, and there is evidence that their virtuoso performances were the centre of attention.

In the fourth century, as in the fifth, we hardly ever see pictures of tragic actors acting: they are depicted in the reality of the parts played. The one vase that is something of an exception is the one with a scene from the *Oedipus Tyrannus* in fig. 20. It was probably made in Syracuse shortly after the mid-fourth century; and in the way it shows the structure of the stage, it owes something to the tradition of painting comic scenes. The moment chosen is interesting. The messenger brings news of the death of Polybos, supposedly Oedipus' father. It is a moment of high drama for the spectator since it begins the process of recognition from which there is no return. Oedipus, in the centre, leans on his stick and by the inclination of his head expresses his concern but no anxiety. Jocasta with hand to cheek shows great distress and indeed foreboding, as does the attendant behind her. So too does the child by Jocasta's legs who senses her mother's alarm and looks round worriedly. The messenger, unusually for such depictions, stands frontally, and although he makes the speaking gesture in their direction, he addresses us, his audience.

A more typical fourth-century scene relating to tragedy is on a Tarentine vase of perhaps the 330s (fig. 21). It relates to the *Hippolytus* of Euripides. In the upper register is a series of divinities including Pan, Apollo, Athena, Aphrodite with Eros, and then Poseidon. Theseus, believing that Hippolytus had seduced his wife Phaedra, invoked Poseidon's curse on him, and he is killed when the horses of his chariot are terrified by a bull from the sea. Here the bull emerges from the bottom of the picture below the horses, and a Fury on the right has a snake in one hand and a flaming torch in the other. On the left is a family retainer who as a messenger will depict the events in narrative (1173–1248). In the fourth-century theatre, such a presentation of an emotionally-charged, disturbing event seems to have been a key role for an actor, and the picture can be seen as a sign of its impact on the audience.

We may compare a scene apparently derived from *Iphigeneia at Aulis* (fig. 22). It gives the highly-charged moment at which Agamemnon, sacrificial knife in hand, is about to kill his daughter Iphigeneia while she, through the intervention of Artemis, is being changed into a deer. That was not seen on the stage; as in the picture derived from *Hippolytus*, narrative is being translated into visual image.

Comparable also is the name vase of the Tarentine Lycurgus Painter (fig. 19), datable shortly before the middle of the fourth century. A retainer stands on the lower left watching the action of Lycurgus, who had been driven mad by Dionysos in revenge for his treatment of his devotee maenads. In the centre Lycurgus, double-axe in his right hand,

grabs his wife by the hair, ready to kill her. She has already fallen and
bleeds from a wound above the breast. On the right two attendants carry
off the body of his son Dryas. Above is a series of gods and, surrounded
by a nimbus, a personification of madness. This again must be a scene
which will be reported and not enacted on stage; it has been suggested,
as was noted above (p. 43), that it is a classic one from a play by
Aeschylus now lost. From an extant play but less precise in its
relationship to an actual stage production is fig. 24, a Paestan vase by the
vase-painter Python of about the middle of the fourth century. It shows
Orestes resting on the *omphalos* at Delphi and speaking with Athena who
will help care for him when he goes to Athens. To the right Apollo
addresses and doubtless warns off one of the Furies who pursued him to
the sanctuary after he had killed his mother Clytemnestra and her lover
Aegisthus. Another of the Furies is seen above, on the higher ground
above the Delphic tripod. The *Oresteia* was already regarded as an old-
style theme in the late fifth century, and by the middle of the fourth such
a vase-painting must have immediately recalled Aeschylus to anyone
looking at it.

The most popular of the classic tragedians with the fourth-century
vase-painters and their customers was Euripides, and we can refer again
here to fig. 25 (again by Python) and to fig. 23 for scenes deriving from
him. These depictions and many others like them are ample testimony
to the status of tragedy in the fourth century. The consistent dress of the
messenger figures suggests that they give us some idea of contemporary
theatrical costume. It is very difficult to say much of the appearance on
stage of other figures since they are represented as the characters created
by the poet. The vases are nevertheless important for the evidence they
provide of the importance of the emotional, even the melodramatic, in
contemporary theatre. The popularity of scenes of this kind is at the
same time evidence of the part that theatre played in the lives of its
audiences.

CHAPTER 7

Menander and the Comedy of Manners

In his *Life of Alexander* (29), Plutarch recounts a remarkable event. On his return to Phoenicia from Egypt early in 331 BC, Alexander organised a major dramatic festival in Tyre. The sponsors were the kings of Cyprus; the actors were the stars of their time; no expense was spared that might win prizes. The event is remarkable for more than that. Greeks thought of such festivals as a traditional civic and religious occasion, part of a local calendar. Here on campaign there was no local tradition. Alexander was entertaining his troops, but also uniting them in an occasion which demonstrated their shared Greek identity. Just as their language, in spite of local dialects, was Greek and not barbarian, so theatre distinguished Greeks from foreigners; and organising a festival at this point in the campaign was surely a deliberate and clever political act.

Alexander perhaps recalled his predecessor Archelaos, who was once host in Macedon to the tragedian Agathon from Athens and to the elderly Euripides, as Hiero of Syracuse had been to Aeschylus. Plutarch specifically mentions dithyrambs and tragedies. Tragedies, as classics known to most of the audience, would have had a special relevance in this setting; comedies are not mentioned, but it would not have been a full festival without them. In any case, this period is the one in which comedy seems to have taken off as the major dramatic genre.

Menander's first play was staged in Athens in 321 BC, and in a career of thirty years he is said to have written just over a hundred. Even though (like Euripides) he won comparatively few victories in his own lifetime, he was (again like Euripides) extremely popular with playgoers and with readers throughout the ancient world. Some plays were perhaps still being staged as late as the fifth century AD, and copies were still being made in the seventh, but at last the line died out, and Menander's influence on modern literature has been felt through the comedies of his Latin followers, Plautus and Terence, who have been more fortunate in their survival. One of the more exciting developments in twentieth-century classical scholarship has been the recovery of substantial parts of his work from papyri.

The appearance on stage of the New Comedy of Menander can be seen in terracottas and other contemporary objects, which also show something of the audience's response to this theatre, what they liked as souvenirs and what it meant in their lives. Statistics make one point clearly: in the seventy-five years or so down to about 325 BC figurines and scenes on pots were dominant, even if depictions of masks were beginning to appear in increasing quantity. In the seventy-five years after 325 BC there are about three times as many masks as figures. In broad terms we may deduce that what had appealed in the earlier period was the comic action on stage and the types who produced it. The terracotta figurines represent favourite figures, just as the pictures on pots depict particularly amusing scenes. Owning a representation of a mask or set of masks implies interest in something rather different, a more complex drama in which the characters represented by the masks interact with each other. The interest is less in the bustle and actuality of the performance than in the complexities of plot and the manipulation of the dramatic action: that is to say in a more subtle and sophisticated comedy.

In the masks themselves we find a greater range of types, with a variety of sub-types to distinguish categories of character. There are, for example, six varieties of young man and at least as many young women, as well as some servant-girls. This reflects the interest in plots concerning the younger generation and their problems in pursuit of their loves.

The audience recognised these masks on sight, whether on or off the stage. This was partly a matter of familiarity and the importance of theatre in contemporary life, but it does have wider implications. This was a period of growing interest in the definition of character (one thinks of Theophrastus' *Characters*), and there were developments in physiognomic theory linking character and appearance. Wavy hair, for example, was taken as a sign of an outgoing character and likened to the mane of a lion. In this same context realistic portraiture was developing.

Masks were taken as physical expressions of the characters they represented. The playwright composed his plot against this background of
visual conventions; and we can sometimes see Menander playing with
the audience's expectations by making a character behave untypically,
like the soldier Polemon in *Perikeiromene* ('The Rape of the Locks'), with
his wavy-haired mask, his sword and military cloak and his violent
temper, who will turn out to be different by nature from the first
impression he makes.

These are the assumptions behind a famous Late Hellenistic composition seen in the marble relief, fig. 44. The detailed interpretation is
much debated but essentially we have an ageing, perhaps drunken,
Dionysos with his retinue of young satyrs and an Old Silenos arriving at
what is perhaps a sanctuary. To the left a comic poet reclines on a couch
and, through his gesture, expresses his wonder at the arrival of the god.
As a comic poet he has a set of masks on the box by his feet, those of a
youth, a girl, a slave and perhaps another slave or an old man.

In reconstructing the Greeks' attitude to theatre, we must remember
that the audience's experience was direct, and unmediated by reviews in
newspapers, magazines, radio or television. Theatre was also their major
source of artificially created images. The images experienced in the

44 *A marble relief:
Dionysos visits a poet.*

theatre were therefore the more compelling and the more clearly remembered. Thus, as we noted above in discussing fifth-century theatre, audiences were keenly aware of one playwright's handling of a motif compared with another's, and playwrights could take advantage of this. The young man at the beginning of Plautus' *Mercator* gives the game away when he says to the audience: 'I'll not do as I've seen other lovers do in comedies, telling their troubles to Night or Day, Sun or Moon . . . it's you I'll tell'. More than once Menander began a play with a lover addressing Night, notably in a famous and recently rediscovered scene of *Misoumenos* ('The Man She Hated'). It is a good question whether this by-play with the convention comes from Plautus or from Menander's rival Philemon, the author of the play Plautus adapted.

45–6 *Masks in miniature:* hetaira *and old man.*

Returning to depictions of masks, we can ask how and where they were used. The terracotta mask of fig. 45 measures about 9 cm from chin

to top of head. It represents the most popular sort of *hetaira* or courtesan, her hair gathered above, with an ivy-wreath as for a party, and the full plump face that people seem to have liked in such girls, in contrast with the thinner, more drawn expressions of the 'better' sort of women. Much of the face colour is lost but there seems to have been black for the brows and eyelashes and red for the hair. Good Athenian girls had black hair. It is a piece which gives an accurate idea of the shape of a mask and it was made either for laying on a flat surface, or for hanging from a wall in a house. The same is true of fig. 46, the mask of an Old Man from comedy.

Fig. 47 is the pendant of a gold earring, a little under 2 cm tall, in the form of an Eros carrying the mask of a slave or old man. An earring with an Eros is an obviously appropriate gift for a woman. What is less clear is why the Eros should hold a mask. The answer may lie in one or both of two directions. In Athens, the place where one normally saw masks, other than in a play, was in the Sanctuary of Dionysos, where they were dedicated to the god after the performance. Masks were therefore in general associated with the sanctuary; the sanctuary was also a place for

47 *A gold earring: Eros with a comic mask.*

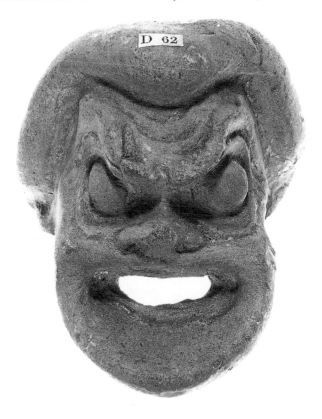

celebration after the play, certainly for the cast (note the Pronomos Vase, fig. 5) and probably for a good number of others. Masks therefore come to be associated with partying, festivity, and good times, and this is particularly true of comic masks, since comedies regularly end in a revel. A good illustration is the Tarentine vase of fig. 43, dating from soon after the middle of the fourth century, where the mask of an Old Man from comedy is shown suspended with a frame of vine. The plant strengthens the association with the god of wine and the product he gave to man. If you gave a party for your friends, it became usual to decorate the room with masks, vine and other garlands, as if to recreate the sanctuary of Dionysos. So it was that masks came naturally to symbolise happiness and the good times; and so we find the mask of an Old Man from comedy used on a cheap mould-made drinking vessel of the earlier part of the second century BC (fig. 48). The theatre takes on a role beyond the theatre, and its images become a part of everyday life.

There was in the period of Menander or very soon afterwards an important series of paintings showing key scenes from his comedies. Our sources make it clear that painting was much the most important art medium of the age, but no original of these paintings survives, nor do we

48 *A mould-made bowl with low-relief comic masks.*

know anything of their context or function: we know of them mostly through copies in other media. One of the best examples is fig. 50, a mosaic made by a Samian called Dioskourides in the later part of the second century BC. It was sold as one of a pre-packaged pair to a man who had it put in the floor of his house in Pompeii. It shows the opening scene (which is also the name-scene) of Menander's *Synaristosai* ('The Hen Party'), of which Plautus made a version in his *Cistellaria*. The mosaic is carefully done and one would guess that it is a good reproduction of the original painting. On the right an old woman in a yellow cloak sits on the end of a couch, an expensive silver drinking cup in her hand. A young girl (without mask) stands in attendance. (There is other evidence that minor figures of this kind did not wear masks.) To her right further along the couch and directly behind the table is a younger woman, a *pseudokore*, also in a yellow cloak. (The *pseudokore*, or 'False Maiden', is a young woman with a secret side to her life; this one has a lover whom she will eventually marry.) At the left of the scene and sitting on a separate stool with elaborate covering is a *hetaira* clutching her hands together. The old woman has a darker face than the other two; her mask is the same

50 *'Such a nice meal I've had . . .': Act I of Menander's* Synaristosai *in a mosaic of* C.100 BC.

as that of the figure in fig. 49. Our illustration shows a modern impression taken from an ancient mould in the Museum's collection, originally from Taranto but most likely copied from an Athenian figurine. It can be dated to the period of Menander. She strides forward, wrapped in her mantle but with the front of her frizzy hair showing, with her head to one side as if talking busily. One sees something of the same character in the mosaic as the old woman bends forward, cup in hand, holding the floor.

A much later version after the same original but largely transposed into mirror-image is to be found among an important series of mosaics found some years ago at Mytilene on the island of Lesbos (fig. 51). They seem to date to the latter half of the fourth century AD, some 450 years

after Dioskourides' version and over 600 years after the original. This version tells us something about the style and appearance of production at that date as well as about the changes in artistic conventions. Unlike the version by Dioskourides, it identifies the play and the act represented, and gives the characters' names: Philainis for the old woman, Plangon for the girl in the middle and Pythias for the call-girl; Plautus has them as Lena ('Procuress'), Selenium and Gymnasium.

The women's party makes a very small group, considering the size of the Athenian stage, and since the scene is presumably set indoors, one wonders if it was not set on the *ekkyklema*, the platform which could be rolled out from the central door (see pp. 38f.). There is other evidence that Menander used it, and it is alluded to in the *Dyskolos* (690, 758).

Paintings like this had an important place in the iconography of the comic theatre. To us it may be surprising that as well as being copied in two-dimensional media such as mosaics, and even gems, they were also converted into three-dimensional versions such as figurines in bronze and clay. Fig. 52 is probably such a case. It is one of a well-known series found in the last century at a site called Myrina on the coast of Asia

52 *The old procurer: a man young men love to hate.*

53 *Slave on an altar:
a moulded vase.*

Minor. This example has replicas in Athens and in the Louvre. It shows a
figure often reproduced in the later part of the Hellenistic period, the
brothel-keeper. He stands with his left leg forward, largely wrapped in
his long mantle. We know from the other examples that his right hand
was raised; the wide grinning mouth and the frowning expression are
typical of the character. By this date the beard is formalised into a
number of corkscrew curls. Our example wears a large, elaborate wreath
with ribbons hanging from it: he must be involved in a party. There are
traces of red-brown colouring for his face, white for his beard, pale blue
for his mantle and yellow for his chiton (the garment below his mantle).

Some dependence on an earlier original, possibly a painting, is also
likely for fig. 53, a figurine used as the basis for a lamp-filler, made in
Campania in the later years of the second century BC. He is a slave seated

on his altar, and although his mask has been fashioned in contemporary style (with semi-circular mouth with distinct, striated edge), his fat rounded legs and his padded belly remind one very much of his Early Hellenistic forebears.

These pieces give us some idea of the importance of recognising iconographic traditions in representations of theatrical material. They give us a clearer idea not only of the formal origins of a particular figure or motif, but of why and how a given motif came to be used in the first place and therefore of the possible range of meanings given to the motif at a particular time and place. Moreover, given the way in which ancient theatre was created, to trace these motifs through the objects means to trace the use of formal motifs on the stage. The figure seated on an altar was, as we have seen, a motif with a long stage history and one that was very variously used as playwrights picked it up and modified it in rivalry with each other. A figure sits on an altar seeking refuge, protected by the god whose altar it is. He cannot be harmed there, even if others find ways to force him off or to deal with him once he leaves that sanctuary. Of course, the figure on the altar can try to negotiate the terms for leaving. Our earliest example is on the mid-fifth century Athenian vase of fig. 15, showing Telephos on the altar with Orestes. As we saw, it seems to reflect Aeschylus; Aeschylus used the altar for Orestes in *Eumenides* (fig. 24), and we see it as a place for brutal sacrifice in what is probably Euripides' *Oineus* (fig. 25); Euripides' version of the Telephos motif was parodied by Aristophanes, both in *Acharnians* in 425 BC and in *Thesmophoriazusae* (fig. 27). Whether or not he was the first to use the motif in comedy we do not know, but scenes on vases and terracotta figurines make it abundantly clear that it became very popular in fourth-century comedy. During the earlier years we find both freemen and slaves on altars, but after the middle of the fourth century the images, at least, are largely confined to slaves. The Athenian figurine in fig. 41 is a good example of the period of transition from so-called Middle to New Comedy. One might guess that the appeal of the motif lay in the slave's defiance of authority (he seems in any case to have become a favourite with the audience), in the dramatic tension between what he wants to do and what may happen to him, and in the suspense as everyone wonders how he will escape dire punishment. Apart from a fragment from his *Perinthia*, we do not have much evidence to show how Menander handled

54–5 *Slaves seated on altars: a bronze figurine and a marble statuette.*

the theme, but one would expect that he did it with a full consciousness of the way others had done it and with unexpected outcomes. The surviving objects suggest that he did it successfully on more than one occasion. Other versions of slaves on altars include figs 53, 54, 55 and 66; they have been selected to show a variety of examples, in different materials, of objects with a range of practical functions.

If we return briefly to the uses of masks, a popular motif from the fourth century onwards was Dionysos holding a mask, and the idea was picked up, probably in 101 BC, by the Athenian mint-magistrates who issued a fine set of silver tetradrachms showing him (figs 56 and 57). Another very popular motif to develop in the Hellenistic period is that of a Muse identified by the mask she holds. Thus on fig. 68 the Muse of

56–7 *(Centre) Coins struck in Athens, probably* 101 BC, *with Dionysos holding masks.*

58–9 *(Below) Roman coins of* 67 BC *with the Muses of Comedy and Tragedy holding masks.*

Tragedy, Melpomene, looks at a tragic mask as a symbol of her craft and the inspiration she gives to playwrights. The Roman Pomponius Musa issued a series of silver coins in 67 BC, decorated (not surprisingly, perhaps) with Muses (figs 58–9), in which Melpomene again holds a tragic mask and her counterpart Thalia has a very large and obvious comic slave mask. It has been thought that they represent a group of statues he had taken as loot from Ambracia. These belong to the Late Hellenistic period, and it is not easy to pin down when the motif began. Fig. 60 shows a fine terracotta figurine, perhaps from Tanagra, of the Early Hellenistic period. A young woman holds a comic mask; but she carries it at her side, almost as a piece of equipment rather than something she cares for; she may be an attendant in a sanctuary, or simply a young woman who holds a mask as a symbol of good fortune.

60 *Boeotian figurine (Tanagra?) of a young woman holding a mask.*

CHAPTER 8

The Traditions of
the Western Theatre

In Book I of Virgil's *Aeneid*, Aeneas, wrapped in a cloud provided by his mother Venus, has a private view of the great works in hand for the building of Dido's Carthage. There are walls to be seen, gates, streets, harbour works; and among all else 'here are others laying deep theatre-foundations, and cutting great columns from the living rock, to adorn the stage that is to be' (427−9). Dido's Carthage prefigures Augustan Rome, or many another city of the provinces, in which a theatre was an emblem of civic pride and imperial magnificence, not unlike some of the great Town Halls of Victorian Britain. We illustrate Orange (figs 61−2) in southern France with its statue of Augustus on the towering façade; we could equally well have chosen its near-twin Aspendos, from the opposite half of the Empire.

These theatres were architecturally brilliant structures, using the Roman techniques of vaulting in concrete to support the seating while at the same time arranging the spaces beneath the vaults as passages for easy entrance and exit. By making the stage building of the same height as the seating and linking the two elements together into a coherent unit, they also, for the first time in western history, made the theatre an enclosed space, a world of its own excluding its surroundings. The only focus for the audience was the stage, or failing that, the façade of the stage-building adorned with statues of the imperial family or other improving and symbolic figures.

While Roman theatres were important instruments of imperial propaganda, it is not always entirely clear what went on in them. There would have been no point in making them into such elaborate structures if they had not attracted large audiences, and there is no suggestion that the Roman plebs would have turned out in large numbers to see a play of

61 Orange: the theatre, mid-first century AD.

62 *Orange: the theatre.*

Euripides, whether in the Greek original or in Latin translation. They had other interests, in jugglers and acrobats, mimes and pantomimes, and in various other sorts of vaudeville performances. For Augustus at the policy-making level, there was some point in decorating his so-called Theatre of Marcellus (13 or 11 BC) with huge marble versions of masks of the Early Hellenistic period of 300 years earlier. It was a recalling of the classical past in the same way that his Forum contained versions of the Caryatids from the Erechtheion on the Athenian Acropolis. The classical past was being used as demonstrating a continuous tradition which made the present respectable and stable.

Something of the same is true of the use of theatrical motifs at the popular level. From the Late Republic and the Early Empire are preserved many carved gems of semi-precious stones decorated with motifs drawn from the stage. We illustrate four examples (figs 63–66).

The mask (fig. 63) is a superb piece, finely carved and with what seems to be an accurate representation of the mask-type of the Flatterer from Comedy. A gem is patently a personal possession, and although we have no way of knowing if its original owner appreciated its accuracy, the maker must have known there was a market for pieces of this quality. There are many others which are much vaguer in their relationship to the actualities of the stage. Doubtless because of the practicalities of scale, gems with depictions of figures are much rarer than those of masks, even if for us they are intrinsically more interesting. The Old Man standing with crook, fig. 64, is a neat sardonyx cameo of some size (2.2 × 1.5 cm). It is remarkably reminiscent of the terracotta figurine from Myrina in Asia Minor, fig. 52. The onyx, fig. 65, has an old man who seems to be in exasperated conversation with his slave; the slave stands relaxed and, by the arrangement of his arms, is pondering what he will say next, what explanation he will make. This too seems to be a motif known from other media. The amethyst, fig. 66, has another popular type deriving from New Comedy, the slave seated on an altar. He appears in many versions. We have already seen the moulded vase, fig. 53. It is earlier, dating to the later part of the second century BC. There is also the small bronze, fig. 54, doubtless designed for table use. He has much the same pondering pose as the standing slave on fig. 65. Then there is the marble statuette, some 62 cm high, fig. 55, of a type which seems to have been particularly popular in Roman houses and gardens. Each of these seated slaves is different and each is known in a number of replicas and in a range of media. One can demonstrate in many cases that they derive from Early Hellenistic originals, most likely paintings of scenes from comedies of Menander in which they were approached by other figures who gave more of the context. One wonders whether, torn from their settings, they still carried with them a knowledge of the particular original play. For the ordinary purchaser, is a seated slave simply a seated slave? Or something more – perhaps in a general way recalling 'classical' theatre, with a connotation of the Dionysiac and the happiness of good times, perhaps as an attractive figure popular from the sort of comedy one remembered learning about at school?

Plays read at school could come at the most elementary level in the form of extracts for copying or repetition. A papyrus manual of the third

63–6 *A group of gems: the mask of the flatterer; old man with a crook; old man and slave; slave on an altar.*

century BC from a Greek school in Egypt, now in the Cairo Museum (65445), has among squares of numbers, proper names of two, three, four and five syllables and other supposedly useful material, a set of passages of literature which include pieces both of tragedy and of comedy. The comic pieces are excerpts from scenes with cooks, perhaps intended to lighten the syllabus, but they remind one that food, feasting and parties are subjects of perennial interest in comedy; and that this interest is well reflected in visual souvenirs of the theatre, such as fig. 42.

Later on in education, students being trained for public speaking, as all educated people were, would be expected to include drama in their reading; verbal devices, speeches, methods of depicting emotion and character could all be read and discussed as models, and it is in this sense that Quintilian recommends Menander in his *Institutio Oratoria* (10.1.69), with specific examples of what he finds admirable, and with a reference to Menander's indebtedness to Euripides.

The actor's art and the orator's overlap: from different periods, one can recall Demosthenes' spiteful contempt for the appearances on stage of his rival Aeschines, and Cicero's observant admiration of Roscius and Aesopus, the great comic and tragic actors of his day. But images of the theatre have power in other ways. In the fourth book of the *Aeneid* (469–73) Virgil describes Dido's terminal despair in a simile which recalls classical tragedy: he remembers the hallucinatory double vision of Pentheus in Euripides' *Bacchae* (918–19), and has blended with that a stage tableau of Orestes haunted by furies somewhat like our fig. 24. The comic stage also created its archetypes. Menander's flatterer in his play *Kolax* is remembered by Plutarch in an essay *On Flattery* for his way of following his master round as well as for what he says; the character survives in a vividly adapted scene in Terence's play *Eunuchus* (391ff.) and in further reminiscences of that. (An acquaintance with this tradition may have prompted the purchase of the gem, fig. 63.) Similarly, a long-lasting image of the lover unable to break with his inconstant partner is taken from Menander's *Eunouchos* by Terence, again in *Eunuchus* (46ff.), and remains as a vivid vignette with dialogue in Horace's *Satires* (2.3.259–71) and in Persius (5.161–75). These memories of famous scenes are in some sense analogous to pictorial representations such as figs 65 and 66; and it is interesting that just as artists can choose to go back beyond their immediate predecessors to an original which seems more authentic, so Persius, instead of following directly on from Terence and Horace, goes back for his characters' names to Menander. Such antiquarianism parallels that of the roughly contemporary painting shown in fig. 67, no doubt a high spot in a favourite comedy, where the slave has bad news for the two lovers, and echoes the role of a tragic messenger like the one in fig. 20.

But how is contemporary to be distinguished from antique? We can move towards an answer by examining the detail of costume and mask and estimating the date of the object independently to check whether its appearance matches what we know of contemporary theatre practice. The object may be using an older prototype, without contemporary reference, and one may then suppose that it was not collected as a souvenir of actual performance. But in a case like the wall-painting of fig. 67, which comes from a house at Pompeii with a collection of similar pieces on its walls, the owner was interested in theatre scenes as such. He

67 'Something awful's
happened': the slave
tells the two lovers his
bad news.

had made sure they were careful and accurate, and they seem to be good
reflections of their originals. Even so, the style of mask and costume is
based on a depiction dating considerably earlier. It is in fact typical of
the final, Flavian phase at Pompeii with its inclination towards antiquarian interest in such things.

Ill-defined as this picture may be in the detail, it accords quite well
with the evidence from literary sources. A key problem here is that it is
hard to distinguish between knowledge of an author based on performance and one based simply on literature. Even when the evidence for
knowledge through performance seems good, it is hard to distinguish
public performances from private, or performances of complete plays
from recitations of famous passages or highlights. Recitation was a
practice which had become increasingly common. Statius, for example,

68 The Muse of
Tragedy, Melpomene,
on a marble base, about
120 BC.

in the *Silvae* (2.1.114), describes a young slave reciting Menander, in a passage where the playwright is admired for his language and the boy for his beauty and a skill which would bring him a victory-crown of roses. The problems are not dissimilar when one tries to assess knowledge acquired by literary means. Does a quotation in itself provide evidence of a love of and deep acquaintance with dramatic literature; or is it based on knowledge of a popular passage, perhaps learned painfully at school, or simply a famous tag, known without context, as many of us know particular lines or phrases of Shakespeare, a commonplace of one's culture?

Given the size and complexity of the Roman world it is hardly surprising that Greek theatre slowly ceased to have the central and formative role it had had in Hellenistic and earlier times. For the western half of the Empire, it represented an alien culture, even if one with great attractions, particularly for the educated upper classes. Nevertheless, dramatic festivals continued to be held in the Greek-speaking half of the Empire – as we know from inscriptional records – and the very fact that the appearance of masks and costumes continued to evolve is itself good evidence for the continued life of the Greek theatre. We can see that tragic masks and tragic costume took on a more and more formalised appearance. The *onkos*, the artificial crown of hair above the forehead, had begun to appear in the earlier part of the Hellenistic period, doubtless as a response to the large theatres and the need to give actors an appearance commensurate with their heroic status even from a distance. In the same way the *kothornos* with platform soles (the 'tragic buskin') was also introduced to give actors added height. The marble relief of about 100 BC from Halikarnassos on the coast of Asia Minor, fig. 68, has a Muse seated and holding a mask. The *onkos* is quite pronounced but the treatment of the beard and hair is still relatively naturalistic. The Muse, as often, takes on some of the characteristics of her speciality and seems to have been given raised soles for her footwear. Something of the same effect may be seen on the coin issued by Pomponius Musa in 67 BC (fig. 59). Fig. 69 gives quite a good idea of the appearance of the mask of a youthful hero in the first century AD, with its arching *onkos*, much more conventionalised locks of hair, wide eyes and open, yawning mouth. By the time of fig. 70 the appearance becomes much more exaggerated. A set of paintings decorating the walls of a house in Ephesos has been

69 *Mask of a young hero of tragedy, 1st century* AD.

taken to date to the later part of the second century, although it would hardly be surprising if they should prove to be later. They are a series of scenes from tragedy and comedy painted on a red ground. The combination of tragic and comic continues a Hellenistic tradition. These are the first such scenes known to us to have labels, and of what may have originally been ten scenes, each about 40–45 cm high, we have *Sikyonioi*, *Oresstes* [sic], *Perikeiromene* and *Iphigeneia*; we illustrate *Orestes*

70 *Two tragic masks on a lamp from North Africa, 2nd/3rd century* AD.

(fig. 71). By this date the tragic actor has become strongly conventionalised, not only in terms of the mask, but with heavy, formal and elaborately decorated costume (looking rather like a bishop dressed for a special occasion), and the boots now have very high platform soles. The actors' capacity for movement was much reduced, largely restricted to gestures of hand and arm while keeping the mask frontal. It is little wonder that Lucian, in his dialogue *Dream or the Cock* (26), records their losing their balance and falling over as a not infrequent occurrence.

Despite the naturalistic character and appearance of the New Comedy of Menander, within the conventions of its day, it is notable that

OPCCCTHC

productions in the period after Menander tended to fossilise. Many of the masks of young women (such as fig. 45) were given hairstyles contemporary with Menander's time, but they kept those same hairstyles in the following centuries, long after they had disappeared from everyday life. The men's masks, similarly, took on a more and more conventional appearance, with stylised hair and corkscrew locks by the ears; the small glass plaques, fig. 72, datable to about the end of the first century AD, provide a striking example. (Compare the treatment on the earlier fig. 63.) The mouths and beards of the older men and the slaves followed a similar pattern (cf. figs 48, 64, 73). The way tragic theatre was played must also have had some effect, but so too must the changed social and

71 *'Would you like to stand up now?': Orestes cared for by Electra in Euripides'* Orestes *(233ff.).*

72 *A pair of glass plaques for inlay, with the mask of an old man.*

political circumstances. By the time of Augustus, the world about which Menander's plays were written had long disappeared. It was becoming as alien to contemporary society as was the world of tragedy. It is hardly surprising, then, that it came to be enjoyed for its text rather than its content.

There can be no doubt, on the other hand, that traditional theatre still held an important position on the scale of cultural values, even in the second century AD and later. Many of the objects we have been considering were quite likely acquired as tokens of culture. The ordinary mass-produced lamps (figs 74 and 75), one with a tragic, the other with a comic mask, clearly gained status from their decoration. Pieces like these were made in northern Italy in the late first and early second century AD and exported over a wide area. The masks depicted are often vague in their relationship to contemporary stage practice: they are

chosen simply as 'tragic' and 'comic' even if ultimately based on known types. It must just have been pleasing to have a motif such as this on one's lamp. In other cases we can go further. We have seen how it became a common practice in the Hellenistic period to use theatrical motifs, and especially those of comedy, as symbolising a happier world, a world of escape from the problems of everyday life. Masks came to be depicted on tomb monuments for just the same reasons. There was also a strong tradition in Roman funerary art of recording and glorifying the activity of the deceased. Often this took the form of presenting the dead as educated, skilled in the arts of the Muses. Thus we have such pieces as the impressive sarcophagus, fig. 76. It was found at Villa Montalto in

73 *Panel in terracotta, with a comic slave mask.*

Rome and was doubtless made in a Roman workshop, even though the marble was imported. It should date to the later part of the third century AD. The Muses stand within arches, each of them distinguished in some way. Polyhymnia, for example, is to be found on the far right in a characteristic leaning pose which is taken from a famous Hellenistic archetype. Melpomene, as Muse of Tragedy, is immediately to the left of centre, sharing an arch with Erato. She has a mask identifiable as that of Herakles with curly hair and beard. Herakles typifies Tragedy in many such monuments: as the favourite tragic hero, and as one who attained divinity through suffering, he appealed to many in that age. It is interesting that the mask's mouth has to some extent become assimilated to that of a comic slave: it demonstrates the vagueness of the reference in the mind of both mason and purchaser. Melpomene also carries the club of Herakles, but by contrast with several similar representations (cf. fig. 68), she does not wear *kothornoi*. Her counterpart immediately to the right of centre, Thalia (sharing with Terpsichore), has a mask which is most probably to be identified as that of a slave or old man.

74–5 North Italian clay lamps with tragic and comic masks.

76 A marble sarcophagus with Muses of Tragedy and Comedy, later 3rd century AD.

77 *A silver casket with Muses, later 4th century* AD*: Euterpe with the double pipe used by accompanists, Thalia with comic mask.*

Near to the end of the story from the ancient world is a superb silver casket (fig. 77). It forms part of the Esquiline Treasure from Rome, having entered the Museum's collections in 1866. It is almost 27 cm high; around its body we again see Muses standing within arches supported by spirally-fluted columns with foliage round about. Its date, however, is as much as a century later than that of the sarcophagus. We are now well into the period when Christianity had become the official

religion of the Roman Empire and the Theatre of Marcellus in Rome was in ruins. Yet these same years also saw a remarkable looking back to the classics of the old world, especially in the Greek-speaking half of the Empire. The Mytilene mosaics (see fig. 51) and some scattered survivals from other centres share this spirit, although with their identifying labels they demonstrate that the interest is an antiquarian one. In Athens there was a short-lived vogue for lamps decorated with quite convincing theatre masks. In Alexandria this is the period of the construction of a theatre (the only one excavated) in what may have been the governor's residential complex. All this was fairly short-lived, but it is worth noting that it is also the period of the originals of the illustrations in the famous Terence manuscript in the Vatican (Lat. 3868) and its kin, with their collections of masks and sketches of scenes – even if, by the standards of our own scholarship, the scribes were not particularly good archaeologists and failed to get many of the details historically accurate.

Among the various means by which the Greek theatre and its images survived, the role of collectors and scholars has so far figured little. The objects we illustrate each have their own history, from creation and first acquisition onwards; they may go through many hands, not least those of excavators, before they end in a collection such as that of the British Museum. Not all are collector's pieces, but the handsome bronze head of Sophocles, fig. 78, came from Istanbul to the collection of the Earl of Arundel before it was eventually acquired by the British Museum. Sometimes little or nothing of the provenance of a piece is known, sometimes (had one but world enough and time) there are involved and interesting stories to tell.

Literary theory in relation to drama is traceable to the beginnings of scientific criticism of literature in the fifth century BC, and reflections of it at a more popular level are to be found in Aristophanes, as in *Frogs* and *Thesmophoriazusae*, which have several times been mentioned in passing above; so has Aristotle, whose seminars not only discussed, among myriad other subjects, poetic composition with special reference to tragedy and comedy, but also dealt with problems in the lists of victors and competitions such as the one illustrated in fig. 11. The work of the scholars of the Alexandrian Library in collecting, collating and commenting on texts was fostered, so we are told, when Demetrios of Phaleron borrowed for the foundation the official archive of plays from

78 Bronze portrait head: Sophocles in old age.

79 The Trackers of Oxyrhynchus: *Sophocles' satyr play* Ichneutai, *a papyrus of the 2nd century* AD.

80 *Euripides'* Hecuba, *with notes, copied by hand soon after* AD 1500.

Athens, and returned copies, not the original manuscripts. Some of this work is reflected in the learned marginal notes to papyri such as fig. 79. Pressure against traditional education, pressure against the performing arts, wars and economic depressions – many of the things which oppress culture still in modern societies – reduced the number of plays available to a small selection from the hundreds once copied and performed; eventually, perhaps from the fifth century AD onwards, the chance of seeing a public performance rapidly descended to nil. The lamp can still be seen burning from our fig. 80, an early sixteenth-century copy of *Hecuba* and *Orestes* by Euripides, two of a triad of plays, the third being *Phoenissae*, which were themselves a selection from a selection; they are

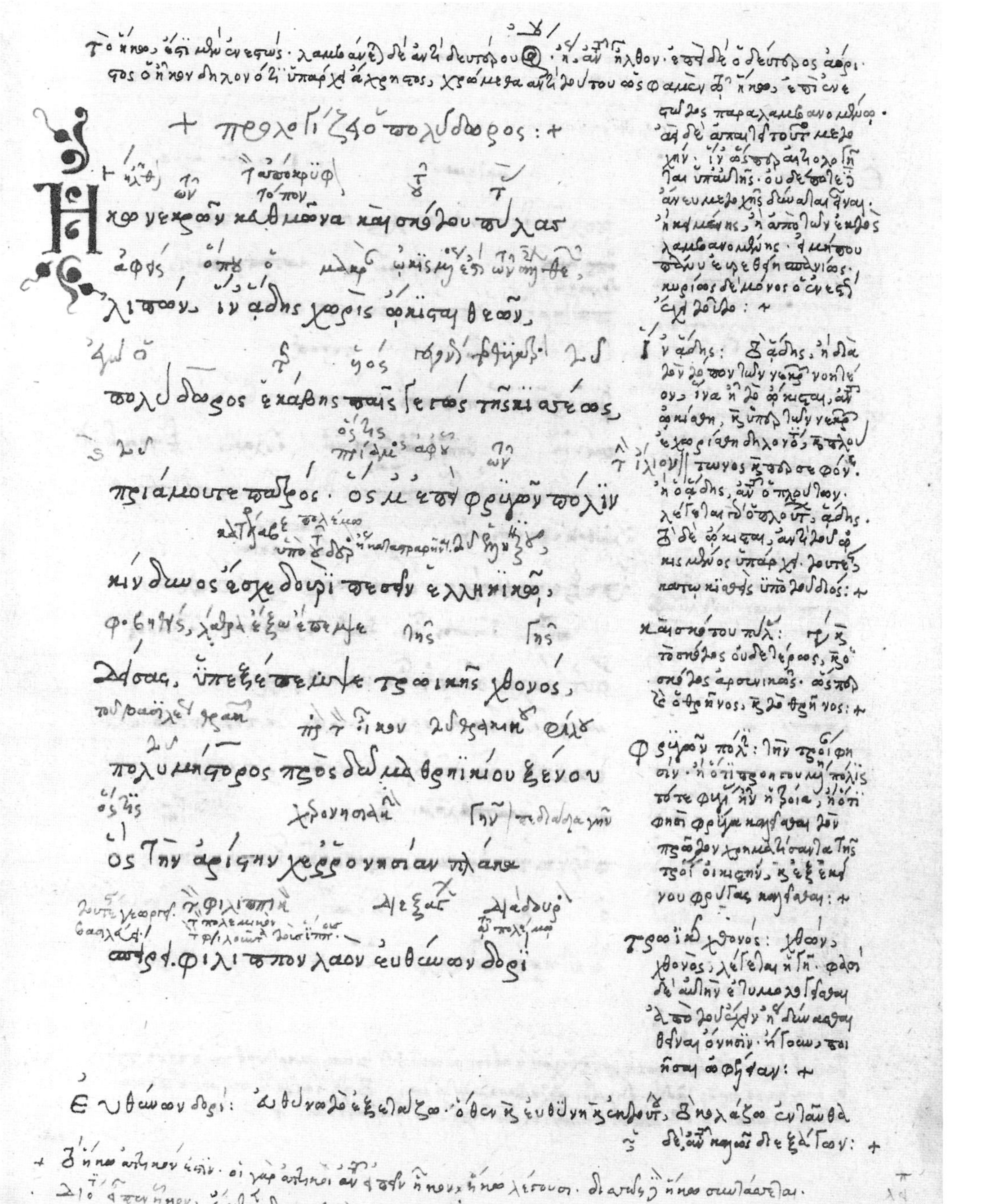

written out with an interlinear construe not unlike that which is now inflicted on school editions of Shakespeare by desperate examination candidates, whose reaction to the notes provided may not be unlike that of Renaissance readers of ancient Greek to notes like those seen here. It was from work on these plays, among his other achievements, that Richard Porson (1759–1808) is remembered as one of the founders of modern scholarship on the surviving texts of Greek drama, and his portrait makes a fitting (and final) fig. 81. The bicentenary of his birth was commemorated in a British Academy lecture given by Denys Page: '. . . the brilliance of that light is revealed in flashes only; but un-mistakable, of indestructible diamond-quality, not to be extinguished or outshone'. One could say the same about the Greek theatre.

81 *Richard Porson (1759–1808).*

Catalogue of Objects Discussed

The list is arranged approximately in the order in which the objects are discussed in the text. The references given are selective and are to standard works of classification and/or particularly relevant discussions. A list of abbreviations follows the catalogue. For ease of consultation, references to *ARV²*, *LCS*, *RVAp* or the like are placed at the end of each bibliographical entry. Penultimate (or, failing the others, last) are the references to the standard listings of theatrical material, *MTS²*, *PhV²*, *MMC³*, or *MNC³*.

All objects, unless otherwise stated, are in the Greek and Roman Department of the British Museum and photographs of them are by courtesy of the Trustees of the British Museum.

1 Corinthian column-krater with padded dancers and Return of Hephaistos; first quarter of the sixth century BC

1867.8-5.860 (B42), from Nola. H. 0.325 m
JHS 85, 1965, 103ff, pl. 23, 2 (Seeberg); A. Seeberg, *Corinthian Komos Vases* (*BICS* Suppl. 27, 1971) no. 227c; D.A. Amyx, *Corinthian Vase-Painting of the Archaic Period* (Berkeley 1988) 234, pl. 102, 2a–b

2 Athenian cup with padded dancers; attributed to the KY Painter, 580–570 BC

1920.2-16.1. H. 0.08 m
ABV 32, 11

3 Athenian black-figure oinochoe with chorus of birds from early comedy; attributed to the Gela Painter, *c.* 480 BC

1842.7-28.787 (B509). H. 0.16 m
Bieber, *Theater²* fig. 123; *IGD* I, 12 (illus. opp. p. 9); Green, *Greek Vases in the J. Paul Getty Museum* 2 (Malibu 1985) 95–118, fig. 11a–c

4 Athenian red-figure calyx krater with A (*above*) Pandora being garlanded, (*below*) piper with four Pans; B (*above*) Piper with seven 'girl' dancers and a male figure, (*below*) maenad with long dress and thyrsos, and satyrs at play; attributed to the Niobid Painter, *c.* 470–460 BC

1856.12-13.1 (E467), from Altamura. H. 0.487 m
Bieber, *Theater²* fig. 16; Pickard-Cambridge, *Dithyramb²*, no. 100, pl. 15a; Pickard-Cambridge, *Festivals²* fig. 42 (drawing); *MTS²* AV17; *ARV²* 601, 23

5 Athenian red-figure volute-krater with the cast of a satyr play in the sanctuary of Dionysos, with the piper Pronomos and the playwright Demetrios; attributed to the Pronomos Painter, end of the fifth century BC

Naples inv. 81673 (H3240), from Ruvo. H. 0.75 m

Bieber, *Theater*[2] figs 31–33; Pickard-Cambridge, *Dithyramb*[2] fig. 49; *IGD* II, 1; *MTS*[2] AV25; *ARV*[2] 1336, 1

6–7 Theatre at Thorikos in coastal Attica

Miller and Cushing, *Papers of the American School of Classical Studies* 4, 1885–86, 1–34; W. Doerpfeld and E. Reisch, *Das griechische Theater* (Athens 1896) 109–111; Hackens, *Thorikos* I, 1963, 105–118 and *Thorikos* III, 1965, 75–96; Gebhard, *Hesperia* 43, 1974, 428–440; *Thorikos and the Laurion in Archaic and Classical Times* (Ghent 1975) 46–47; Pöhlmann, *Museum Helveticum* 38, 1981, 137–8

Earliest construction dated to late sixth century; further work in the Classical period (including construction of the small Temple of Dionysos at the side of the playing area); further modifications after the middle of the fourth century BC

8 Athenian red-figure rhyton with satyr choreut wreathed, in shaggy drawers; later fifth century BC

1846.9-25.16 (E790), from Nola. H. 0.24 m
CVA (4) pll. 37, 5 and 38, 3; Bieber, *Theater*[2] fig. 26; *MTS*[2] AV29; *ARV*[2] 908, Group W, no. 1

9 Athenian red-figure cup with (A) satyrs pursuing Iris, (B) satyrs attacking Hera; attributed to the Brygos Painter, *c.* 490–480 BC

1873.8-10.376 (E65), from Capua. H. 0.275 m
Simon, *Eye of Greece* pl. 30; *ARV*[2] 370, 13 and 1649, *Paral.* 365, *Addenda*[2] 224

10 Lucanian red-figure calyx-krater with the companions of Odysseus manhandling the tree with which to blind the drunken Polyphemos; satyrs dancing forward from the right (Euripides, *Cyclops*); attributed to the Cyclops Painter, *c.* 415–410 BC

1947.7-14.18. H. 0.47 m

Brommer, *Satyrspiele*[2] 19–21, figs 11–12; *IGD* II, 11; *RVSIS* fig. 9; *MTS*[2] 157; *LCS* 27 no. 85

11 Inscription on marble recording victors in the competitions at Athens
Athens, Epigraphical Museum

IG II[2], 2318 col. 2; Pickard-Cambridge, *Festivals*[2] 104; H.-J. Mette, *Urkunden dramatischer Aufführungen in Griechenland* (Berlin – New York 1977) 13, 84

12 Cast of marble relief from Monument of Lysikrates in Athens: Dionysos, satyrs and pirates (dithyramb with boys' chorus), 334 BC. H. 0.25 m

J. Stuart and N. Revett, *The Antiquities of Athens* i (London 1762) 27–34; *Cat. Sculpture*, i, pp. 248–257 no. 430; Bieber, *Theater*[1] fig. 10; [2]fig. 18; J. Travlos, *Pictorial Dictionary of Ancient Athens* (London 1971) 348; H. Bauer, 'Lysikratesdenkmal, Baubestand und Rekonstruktion', *Athenische Mitteilungen* 92, 1977, 204–227; Ridgway, *Hell.Sc.* 15–17; *MTS*[2] AS8

Known in the 17th century as the Lantern of Demosthenes, this victory monument had remained relatively undamaged since Antiquity. The view illustrated is from C. Wordsworth, *Athens and Attica: Notes of a Tour* (3rd ed. London 1855), facing p. 131. Christopher Wordsworth (1807–1885), nephew of the poet, travelled in Greece in his twenties and produced the popular travel books with their engravings from which many in the Victorian age formed their image of the country's classical past. He was well known in his time as a classical scholar and theologian, and became Bishop of Lincoln in 1869

13–14 Theatre of Dionysos at Athens

E. Fiechter, *Das Dionysos-Theater in Athen* (Stuttgart 1935–1950); A.W. Pickard-Cambridge, *The Theatre of Dionysus in Athens* (Oxford 1946); J. Travlos, *Pictorial Dictionary of Ancient Athens*

(London 1971) 537–550; Newiger, *Wiener Studien* 89 (ns 10), 1976, 80–92; Pöhlmann, *Museum Helveticum* 38, 1981, 129–146; Townsend, *Hesperia* 55, 1986, 421–438

Initial date of any formal construction uncertain; major stage building perhaps in later fifth century, important re-modelling in third quarter of fourth century; many later modifications, e.g. under Nero and a thorough reconstruction of stage building under Hadrian; reduced to much smaller size and present stage probably under Constantine

15 Athenian red-figure pelike with Telephos holding Orestes on the altar, Agamemnon approaching (Aeschylus, *Telephos*); attributed to an imitator of the Chicago Painter, *c.* 450 BC

1836.2-24.28 (E382). H. 0.327 m
Séchan 127; Csapo, *Quaderni Urbinati di Cultura Classica* 34, 1990, 41–52; *ARV²* 632

16 Athenian red-figure kantharos with Ixion condemned to the wheel (Aeschylus, *Ixion*); attributed to the Amphitrite Painter, *c.* 460–450 BC

1865.1-3.23 (E155), from Nola. H. 0.238 m
CVA (4) pl. 33, 2 and pl. 35, 2; Séchan fig. 115; *JhOAI* 42, 1955, 4–26 (Simon); *LIMC* v (1990), *s.v.* Ixion; *ARV²* 832, 37

17 Athenian red-figure hydria with Andromeda being tied to the stakes (Sophocles, *Andromeda*); attributed to the workshop of the Coghill Painter, 450–440 BC

1843.11-3.24 (E169), from Vulci. H. 0.456 m
CVA (5) pll. 75, 1 and 76; Séchan 149, fig. 47; *IGD* III.2, 3; Green, *GRBS* 32, 1991, 42–44; *MTS²* 117, AV56; *ARV²* 1062, 1681

18 Athenian red-figure neck-amphora with Phineus blind, his food stolen by Harpies; attributed to the Nikon Painter, *c.* 470–450 BC

1864.10-7.82 (E302). H. 0.334 m
CVA (5) pl. 53, 2; *IGD* III.1, 25; J.M. Padgett, *JMFA Boston* 3, 1991, 15–33; *MTS²* 144; *ARV²* 652, 2

19 Tarentine red-figure calyx-krater: (*above*) gods, Fury with nimbus, altar; (*below*) old man with stick in tragic costume; youth, Lycurgus attacking his wife, servants with body of son (Aeschylus, *Edonoi*). Attributed to the Lycurgus Painter, mid-fourth century BC

1849.6-23.48 (F271), from Ruvo. H. 0.585 m
Séchan, fig. 21; *IGD* III.1, 15; *MTS²* 128, TV46; *RVAp* i, 415–16 no. 16/5, pl. 147

See M.L. West, *Studies in Aeschylus* (Stuttgart 1990) 31

20 Sicilian red-figure calyx-krater with scene from Sophocles, *Oedipus Tyrannus*: the arrival of the messenger with the news of the death of Oedipus' father, Polybos; Jocasta and the children stand near Oedipus and there is an attendant to the right. Attributed to the Capodarso Painter; third quarter of the fourth century BC

Syracuse 66557, from Syracuse. Pres. H. 0.24 m
IGD III.2, 8; Bertino, *Archaeologica. Scritti in onore di A. Neppi Modona* (Florence 1975) 25–27, fig. 4; *LIMC* i (1981) 820 no. 1, pl. 659 (*s.v.* Antigone); *LCS* Suppl. i, 105

21 Tarentine red-figure volute-krater with Hippolytus crashing on the sea-shore (Euripides, *Hippolytus*); attributed to the Darius Painter, third quarter of the fourth century BC; foot restored

1856.12-26.1 (F279). H. 0.658 m
Séchan fig. 99; *IGD* III.3,24; Linant de Bellefonds, *LIMC* v (1990) 458 no. 105, pl. 325; J.H. Oakley, '"The Death of Hippolytus" in South Italian Vase-Painting', *NumAntCl* 20, 1991, 63–83; *MTS²* 158; *RVAp* ii, 487 no. 18/17, pl. 173, 1

22 Tarentine red-figure volute-krater with the
sacrifice of Iphigeneia (Euripides, *Iphigeneia
at Aulis*); from the workshop of the Iliupersis
Painter, second quarter of the fourth century
BC

   1865.1-3.21 (F159), from the Basilicata.
   H. 0.705 m
   Séchan fig. 108; Arias, *Boll.Ist.naz. del Dramma
   antico* 1930, 89–96; Kahil and Icard, *LIMC* v
   (1990) 712 no. 11, pl. 467; *MTS*² 159; *RVAp* i,
   204 no. 8/104

23 Campanian red-figure neck-amphora with
woman (Antigone) and paidagogos (Euripides, *Phoenissae*); attributed to the Ixion
Painter, third quarter of the fourth century
BC

   1867.5-8.1337 (F338). H. 0.522 m
   CVA pl. 7, 6; *Archäologischer Anzeiger* 1976, 221,
   figs 12–13; *MTS*² 162; *LCS* 339 no. 797

24 Paestan red-figure bell-krater with Athena,
Orestes on the altar, Apollo, two Furies,
Clytemnestra (or Leto) and Pylades (? or
Hermes) above (cf. Aeschylus, *Eumenides*);
by Python, *c.* 350–340 BC

   1917.12-10.1. H. 0.565 m
   Bieber, *Theater*² fig. 97; *IGD* III.1, 11; *RVP* 145
   no. 244, pl. 91

25 Paestan red-figure hydria with king and
woman approaching bound man on altar
(Euripides, *Oineus?*); by Python, third
quarter of the fourth century BC

   1772.3-20.37 (F155). H. 0.44 m
   Pickard-Cambridge, *Festivals*¹ fig. 189; Trendall, *Paestan Pottery*, no. 154, pl. 16b; *IGD* III.
   3, 41; *MTS*² PV3; *RVP* 149 no. 249, pl. 94a–b

26 Plain-ware oinochoe decorated in poly-
chrome technique with a man rowing a fish;
late fifth century BC

   1898.2-27.1, probably from Athens.
   H. 0.245 m
   Hesperia 24 (1955) pl. 37a (Crosby); Bieber,

*Theater*² fig. 210; *PhV*² no. 9; Pickard-
Cambridge, *Festivals*² fig. 87; *IGD* IV, 5; *MMC*³
AV10
Has been associated with Eupolis, *Taxi-
archoi*: see Kassel–Austin, *Poetae Comici
Graeci* v (1986) 452–66

27 Tarentine red-figure bell-krater with scene
of Telephos parody (Aristophanes, *Thesmophoriazusae*); attributed to the Schiller
Painter, *c.* 380–370 BC

   Würzburg H 5697. H. 0.185 m.
   A. Kossatz-Deissmann in H.A. Cahn and E.
   Simon (eds), *Tainia. Festschrift Roland Hampe*
   (Mainz 1980) 281–290, pl. 60; *RVSIS* ill. 109;
   Phoenix 40, 1986, 372–392 (Csapo); *Proceedings
   of the Cambridge Philological Society* 213 (ns 33),
   1987, 92–104 (Taplin); *RVAp* i, 65 no. 4/4a

28 Tarentine red-figure bell-krater with scene
of the old man Cheiron being pushed up
onto the stage, Nymphs looking on; attributed to the McDaniel Painter, *c.* 380–
370 BC

   1849.6-20.13 (F151). H. 0.374 m
   IGD IV, 35; Bieber, *Theater*² fig. 491; *PhV*²
   no. 37; *RVAp* i, 100 no. 4/252

29 Paestan red-figure bell-krater with old man
dragging slave by the wrist; the slave carries
phiale, fillet and situla; attributed to
Python, third quarter of the fourth century
BC

   1873.8-20.347 (F189), from Capua. H. 0.4 m
   Bieber, *Theater*² fig. 517; *IGD* IV, 17; *PhV*²
   no. 39; *RVP* 159 no. 280, pl. 103a–b

30 Tarentine red-figure skyphos with man at a
girl's door; attributed to the Wellcome
Group, second quarter of the fourth century
BC

   1849.5-18.15 (F124). H. 0.203 m
   Bieber, *Theater*² fig. 500; *JhOAI* 54, 1983, 66
   fig. 7; *PhV*² no. 94; *RVAp* i, 304 no. 11/182a

31 Paestan red-figure bell-krater with scene of two men, one climbing ladder to woman at window while the other stands by holding torch, wreath and situla; attributed to Asteas, soon after the middle of the fourth century BC

1865.1-3.27 (F150). H. 0.378 m
Bieber, *Theater*[2] fig. 501; *PhV*[2] no. 36; *RVP* 72 no. 45, pl. 28a–b

32–33 Theatre at Epidauros. Later fourth century BC

A. von Gerkan and W. Müller-Wiener, *Das Theater von Epidauros* (Stuttgart 1961); L. Polacco, *NumAntCl* 7, 1978, 83–93; L. Käppel, *JdI* 104, 1989, 83–106

Initial phase, lower part of seating, perhaps envisaged second phase, upper part of seating, which was eventually constructed *c.* 170–160 BC.

34 Athenian terracotta figurine of Herakles standing with club and lionskin, his bow and quiver in his left hand. Earlier part of the fourth century BC

1842.7-28.752, from Melos. H. 0.09 m
Pickard-Cambridge, *Festivals*[1] fig. 82; Higgins i, no. 741, pl. 98; *MMC*[3] AT 26b

35 Athenian terracotta figurine of traveller with *pilos*, flask and basket, and wearing a cloak which is fastened at the neck and drawn over the top of the *pilos*. Late fifth or early fourth century BC

1880.11-13.3, said to be from Tanagra. H. 0.09 m
Pickard-Cambridge, *Festivals*[1] fig. 123; Higgins i, no. 738, pl. 98; *MMC*[3] AT 6b

36 Athenian terracotta figurine of nurse holding baby on left arm. Late fifth or early fourth century BC

1865.7-20.37 (TC747; C4), said to be from Athens. H. 0.075 m

Pickard-Cambridge, *Festivals*[1] fig. 141; Higgins i, no. 747, pl. 99; *MMC*[3] AT 9b

37 Athenian terracotta figurine of young woman raising her mantle before her face, as if to hide. Late fifth or early fourth century BC

1907.5-18.7. H. 0.095 m
Pickard-Cambridge, *Festivals*[1] fig. 140; Higgins i, no. 744, pl. 99; *MMC*[3] AT 10c

38 Corinthian terracotta figurine of standing man with arms outstretched. Head moulded; body handmade. First half of the fourth century BC

1867.2-5.22, from Corinth. H. 0.12 m
Higgins i, no. 963, pl. 135; Higgins, *Terracottas*, pl. 36d; *MMC*[3] CT 2

39 Athenian terracotta figurine of young woman wearing stephane, left hand to hip, right hand to left shoulder. Third quarter of the fourth century BC

1865.7-20.43 (C5), probably from Athens. H. 0.14 m
Higgins i, no. 746, pl. 98; Higgins, *Terracottas* pl. 31a; *MMC*[3] AT 114

40 Athenian terracotta figurine of young woman standing with head to one side (red on lips, chiton and shoes; blue on himation). Third quarter of the fourth century BC

1907.5-20.79b, said to be from Olbia. H. 0.09 m
Higgins i, no. 745, pl. 99; Pickard-Cambridge, *Festivals*[1] fig. 142; Bieber, *Theater*[1] fig. 161; *MMC*[3] AT 115

41 Athenian terracotta figurine of slave sitting on altar, right hand to head (traces of red on face, beard, hands and feet). 330–310 BC

1879.3-6.5, from Piraeus (?). H. 0.13 m
Pickard-Cambridge, *Festivals*[1] fig. 132; Higgins i, no. 743, pl. 98; Bieber, *Theater*[2] fig. 148; *MMC*[3] AT 111d, pl. Va

42 Tarentine calyx-krater in the Gnathia technique with slave-caterer carrying table with cake, in a sanctuary; attributed to the Compiègne Painter, mid-fourth century BC

1856.12-26.112 (F543), from Fasano. H. 0.284 m
CVA (1) pl. 2 (38), 2; Bieber, *Theater*[2] fig. 527; *PhV*[2] no. 178

43 Tarentine kantharoid krater in the Gnathia technique with mask of Old Man from Comedy suspended within vine; attributed to the Compiègne Painter, mid-fourth century BC

1856.12-26.113 (F548), from Fasano. H. 0.250 m
CVA (1) pl. 2(38); *PhV*[2] no. 181; *MMC*[3] TV 5

44 Marble relief with Dionysos visiting a comic poet (four comic masks on a low platform) (a number of the details restored). Perhaps early first century AD after an earlier (second century BC?) original

1805.7-3.123. 0.915 × 1.51 m
Cat. Sculpture iii, no. 2190; Th. Schreiber, *Hellenistische Reliefbilder* (1894) pl. 37; Picard, *AJA* 38, 1934, 140 fig. 2; Handley, *JHS* 93, 1973, pl. 2; B. Hundsalz, *Das dionysische Schmuckrelief* (Munich 1987) 148, K 24 (ill.); *MNC*[3] 3AS 4a

45 Terracotta miniature mask of young woman (*hetaira*) wearing ivy wreath (red on hair, black on brows and eyelashes); earlier third century BC

1856.8-26.243, from Kalymnos. H. 0.091 m
Walters, *Terracottas* 234 no. C 469; *MNC*[3] 1AT 75a

46 Campanian terracotta miniature mask of Old Man from Comedy. Perhaps later third century BC

1873.8-20.565, from Capua. H. 0.082 m

Walters, *Terracottas* 308 no. D 62; *MNC*[3] 1AT 37h

47 Gold earring pendant: Eros carrying mask of slave or old man. 325–250 BC

1856.12-26.1378. H. 0.018 m
Marshall, *Jewellery* no. 1898, pl. 32; *MNC*[3] 1DA 7

48 Athenian mould-made relief bowl: in frieze on upper wall, series of Old Man masks linked by festoons; about 200 BC

1927.7-14.2. H. 0.09 m
MNC[3] 2AV 30a

49 Tarentine terracotta mould (an impression shown) of woman moving forward; about 300 BC

1887.7-25.7, from Taranto. Pres. H. 0.13 m
Walters, *Terracottas* 438 no. E 31; Bieber, *Theater*[2] fig. 354; Pickard-Cambridge, *Festivals*[1] fig. 144; *MNC*[3] 1AT 24

50 Floor mosaic signed by Dioskourides of Samos: opening scene of Menander, *Synaristosai* 'Women at Breakfast'; late second century BC after an original of *c.* 300 BC

Naples 9987, from Pompeii, 'Villa of Cicero'. H. 0.42 m
Bieber, *Theater*[1] fig. 242, [2]fig. 347; Pickard-Cambridge, *Theatre of Dionysus* (Oxford 1946) fig. 86; *IGD* 145, V,1, colour plate facing p. 8 (with 51 below); *MNC*[3] 3DM 1

51 Mosaic floor-panel with scene from Menander, *Synaristosai*. After the middle of the fourth century AD

Mytilene, House of the Menander. H. *c.*0.7 m
S. Charitonides, L. Kahil, R. Ginouvès, *Les mosaïques de la Maison du Ménandre à Mytilène* (*AntK* Beiheft 6, Basle 1970) pl. 5, 1 (colour); *IGD* V, 2, colour-plate facing p. 8 (with 50 above); *MNC*[3] 6DM 2.3

52 Terracotta figurine of old procurer (*pornoboskos*) standing and holding a garland in his right hand (traces of red on face, pale blue on mantle, yellow on chiton, white on beard). Later second century BC

1893.9-15.5, from Myrina. H. 0.192 m
Walters, *Terracottas* 242, C 520; *MNC*[3] 3DT 3b

53 Campanian moulded vase in the form of a slave seated on an altar (red on face and sandals, blue on fillet, brown on hair). Later second century BC

1873.10-20.2, from Italy? H. 0.119 m
Walters, *Terracottas* D 322, pl. 34; Pickard-Cambridge, *Festivals*[1] fig. 130; Bieber, *Theater*[2] fig. 411; *BM Yearbook* 1 (1976) 18 no. 10, figs 11–12, pl. 1 (colour); *MNC*[3] 3NV 6

54 Bronze figurine of slave seated with one hand to face. Probably early first century AD

1878.5-4.1. H. 0.112 m
Walters, *Bronzes*, no. 1626; Bieber, *Theater*[1] fig. 210, [2]fig. 406; *MNC*[3] 4XB 9

55 Marble statuette of slave seated on altar (the legs from the knees to the ankles restored, as is the right forearm to the wrist)

1805.7-3.45, from Rome, Villa Fonsega (Celio). H. 0.62 m
Cat. Sculpture iii, no. 1767; Bieber, *Theater*[1] fig. 232, [2]fig. 558; *MNC*[3] 4XS 4a (with refs)

56–57 Athenian silver tetradrachms issued by mint-magistrates Timostratos and Poses, months I–K of the year (most probably) 101 BC: Dionysos holding masks

M. Thompson, *The New Style Silver Coinage of Athens* (1961) Type 830c; *MNC*[3] 3AC 1 and *MTS*[2] 111, AC 1

58 Roman silver denarius with Muse of Comedy (Thalia) standing and holding a large slave mask in her right hand. One of a series with Muses issued by Pomponius Musa, 67 BC

E.A. Sydenham, *The Coinage of the Roman Republic* (London 1952) no. 821, pl. 23; Webster, *Hell. Art* 58f., pl. 16; J.P.C. Kent, *Roman Coins* (1978) 269 no. 58, pl. 16; *MNC*[3] 3RC 1

59 Roman silver denarius with Muse of Tragedy (Melpomene) standing with club and wearing lion-skin, mask (of Herakles) in left hand. Same issue as 58 above

E.A. Sydenham, *The Coinage of the Roman Republic* (London 1952) no. 816, pl. 23; Webster, *Hell. Art* 58f., pl. 16; *MTS*[2] 93, IC 1

60 Boeotian terracotta figurine of young woman holding mask in right hand; probably earlier part of the third century BC

1884.2-23.5, from Tanagra (?). H. 0.212 m
Walters, *Terracottas* 219, C 309; Pickard-Cambridge, *Festivals*[2] fig. 133; Webster, *Hell. Art* 52, pl. 13 (colour); R. Higgins, *Tanagra and the Figurines* (1987) 140, fig. 168; *MNC*[3] 1BT 29

61–62 Theatre at Orange. Mid-first century AD

E.R. Fiechter, *Die baugeschichtliche Entwicklung des antiken Theaters* (Munich 1914) fig. 78 (whence our drawings); D.S. Robertson, *Handbook of Greek and Roman Architecture* (Cambridge 1945) 279–282 (compared with Aspendos); E. Frézouls, *Aufstieg und Niedergang der römischen Welt*, ii 12.1 (Berlin, New York 1982) 343–441 (for general background); G. Bejor, *Athenaeum* 57, 1979, 126–138 (social and political role of Early Imperial theatres)

One of the best preserved Roman theatres; typically Roman in its closed form and imposing stage building (36 × 103 m); statue of Augustus in the main central niche; seating for *c.* 7000, part resting on the hillside, part free-standing; constructed within a larger recreation complex

63 Gem (sard) with mask of the Flatterer; perhaps mid-first century BC–mid-first century AD

1872.6-4.1204. 12 × 10 mm
Walters, *Gems* no. 2199; *MNC*[3] 4XJ 76a

64 Sardonyx cameo with old man standing with crook, frontal; probably early Imperial

1872.6-4.1327. 22 × 15 mm
Walters, *Gems* no. 3630, pl. 42; *MNC*[3] 4XJ 10g

65 Gem (onyx) with old man with crook confronting slave with arms folded, right hand to chin; perhaps mid-first century BC–mid-first century AD

1867.5-7.613. 12 × 8 mm
Walters, *Gems* no. 2192, pl. 27; Lippold pl. 60, 4; *MNC*[3] 4XJ 3c

66 Gem (amethyst) with slave seated on altar, his arms folded; perhaps mid-first century BC–mid-first century AD

1867.5-7.612. 12 × 9 mm
Walters, *Gems* no. 2184, pl. 27; *MNC*[3] 4XJ 30

67 Wall-painting with scene from comedy: old slave rushing on with news to an apprehensive youth and girl. Third quarter of the first century AD

Pompeii I.vi.11, Casa dei Quadretti Teatrali. 0.51 × 0.475 m
Bieber, *Theater*[1] fig. 524, [2]fig. 395; Csapo, *Antike Kunst* 36, 1993, pl. 11, 4; *MNC*[3] 5NP 5a

Perhaps Philemon, *Phasma*: cf. Plautus, *Mostellaria* 348ff.

68 Circular marble base decorated in relief with the nine Muses: seated tragic Muse (Melpomene) holding mask with long straggly hair and beard, raised brows, high onkos, roll in her left hand and wearing kothornoi. Perhaps about 120 BC

1868.4-5.159/1868.6-20.30, from Halikarnassos. H. 0.82 m
Cat. Sculpture iii, no. 1106; A. Trendelenburg, *Der Musenchor: Relief einer Marmorbasis aus Halikarnass* (Berliner Winckelmannsprogramm 36, 1876); Webster, *Gr. Bühnenaltertümer* (Göttingen 1963) pl. 4b; D. Pinkwart, *Antike Plastik* 6,

1967, 89–94, pll. 53–57; Ridgway, *Hell.Sc.* 258, ill. 32; *MTS*[2] ZS 1, pl. 3b

The base supported a metal object of uncertain form. The Muses on this piece are often compared with those on the Museum's Archelaos Relief from Bovillae in Central Italy: *Cat. Sculpture* iii, no. 2191; C. Watzinger, *Das Relief von Archelaos von Priene* (63. *BWPr*, 1903); D. Pinkwart, *Antike Plastik* 4, 1965, 55–65, pll. 28–35; Ridgway, *Hell.Sc.* pl. 133. It dates to the late third or second century and Melpomene there too has high-soled kothornoi and carries a mask with high onkos

69 Marble relief with mask of young male with sword and drapery below; perhaps first century AD

1805.7-3.146. H. 0.18 m
Cat. Sculpture iii, 2450, fig. 57; *MTS*[2] IS 2

70 North African clay lamp with two tragic masks within frame: curly-haired, bearded man with onkos; unbearded mask with high onkos of barley-sugar vertical locks; c. 175–250 AD

1836.2-24.466. L. 0.091 m
Walters, *Lamps* 760, fig. 140; D.M. Bailey, *A Catalogue of the Lamps in the British Museum* iii (London 1988) no. Q 1716, pl. 15; *MTS*[2] FL 1, pl. 6b

71 Wall-painting of scene labelled as being from the *Orestes* of Euripides; later second century AD

Ephesos, 'Hanghaus 2'. H. c. 0.4 m
V.M. Strocka, *Die Wandmalerei der Hanghäuser in Ephesos* (Forschungen in Ephesos VIII.1, Vienna 1977) 48 no. 65 (ill.)

72 Pair of matching glass half-plaques (for inlay) with mask of Old Man from Comedy; later first or second century AD

1897.5-11.112 (29396). H. 0.028 m

D.B. Harden *et al.*, *Masterpieces of Glass* (1968) 26 no. 22; *MNC*³ 4EG 1b

73 Central Italian terracotta decorative panel with mask of comic slave, from a series having sets of three in arched frames; perhaps first half of the first century AD

1805.7-3.431, from Italy. Pres. H. 0.10 m
Walters, *Terracottas* 414, D 658; *MNC*³ 4RT 13b

74 North Italian clay lamp with the stamp of the lamp-maker FORTIS: tragic mask. Last quarter of the first century AD

1856.7-1.337. L. 0.109 m
D.M. Bailey, *A Catalogue of the Lamps in the British Museum* ii (London 1980) no. Q 1164 PRB, pl. 51

75 North Italian clay lamp with mask of comic slave; late first–early second century AD

1814.7-4.178. L. 0.102 m
D.M. Bailey, *A Catalogue of Lamps in the British Museum*, ii (London 1980) no. Q 1169, pll. 52 and 96; *MNC*³ 5RL 23a

76 Sarcophagus of Proconnesian marble with Muses of Tragedy with mask (curly hair on low onkos, swinging brows, slave mouth: Herakles) and of Comedy with mask of slave or old man; later third century AD

1805.7-3.120, from Villa Montalto, Rome. H. 0.725 m
Cat. Sculpture iii, 316 no. 2305; S. Walker, *Catalogue of Roman Sarcophagi* (London 1990) no. 24, pl. 9 (with refs); *MTS*² IS 35; *MNC*³ 6RS 25c

Probably completed in Rome from an imported rough

77 Silver casket decorated with the Muses in architecturally defined niches, as in a building. Later fourth century AD

(Medieval & Later Antiquities) 1866.12-29.2,

from Rome, Esquiline. H. 0.267 m
O.M. Dalton, *Catalogue of Early Christian Antiquities* (London 1901) 64 ff., no. 305, pl. 19; K.J. Shelton, *The Esquiline Treasure* (London 1981) 75 ff., no. 2, pl. 15; *MNC*³ 6RA 1

78 Lifesize bronze portrait head of Sophocles

1760.9-19.1, formerly in the collection of the Earl of Arundel (purchased in Constantinople at the beginning of the 17th century). H. 0.348 m
Walters, *Bronzes* no. 847; G.M.A. Richter, *The Portraits of the Greeks*, i (London 1965) 131, Type IV.1, figs 708–710

79 Papyrus with text of Sophocles, *Ichneutai*. Second century AD

British Library, Papyrus 2068
POxy 9.1174 (Hunt); Pack² 1473; Turner, *Greek Manuscripts of the Ancient World*² (London 1987) no. 34

80 Manuscript of Euripides, *Hecuba* lines 1–9, with interlinear construe and commentary. Early 16th century AD

British Library, Harley 5725, folio 141, recto
A. Turyn, *The Byzantine Manuscript Tradition of the Tragedies of Euripides* (Urbana 1957) 208 ff. and pl. XXI ('written probably by Andreas Donus')

81 Richard Porson (1759–1808). Engraved by C. Turner, from a painting by T. Kirby in the possession of the Revd Dr E.D. Clarke [and now in Trinity College, Cambridge] Trinity College, Cambridge

Published 1 October 1812 by R. Harraden & Son, Cambridge [and reproduced here from a copy in Trinity College by courtesy of the Master and Fellows]

C.O. Brink, *English Classical Scholarship* (Cambridge, James Clark, 1986) 99–113; Denys Page, 'Richard Porson (1759–1808)', *Proceedings of the British Academy* 45, 1959, 221–236

Abbreviations used in the Catalogue

ABV	J.D. Beazley, *Attic Black-Figure Vase-Painters* (Oxford 1956)
AJA	*American Journal of Archaeology*
ARV²	J.D. Beazley, *Attic Red-Figure Vase-Painters* (Oxford 1963)
Bieber, *Theater*	M. Bieber, *History of the Greek and Roman Theater* (Princeton, 1st edn 1939, 2nd edn 1961)
BICS	*Bulletin of the Institute of Classical Studies*
Cat. *Sculpture*	A.H. Smith, *A Catalogue of Sculpture in the Department of Greek and Roman Antiquities, British Museum*, i (London 1892); ii (London 1900); iii (London 1904)
CVA	*Corpus Vasorum Antiquorum*
GRBS	*Greek, Roman and Byzantine Studies*
Higgins i	R.A. Higgins, *Catalogue of the Terracottas in the Department of Greek and Roman Antiquities, British Museum*, i (London 1954)
IGD	A.D. Trendall and T.B.L. Webster, *Illustrations of Greek Drama* (London 1971)
JdI	*Jahrbuch des Deutschen Archäologischen Instituts*
JhOAI	*Jahreshefte des Oesterreichisches Archäologischen Instituts in Wien*
JHS	*Journal of Hellenic Studies*
LCS	A.D. Trendall, *The Red-Figured Vases of Lucania, Campania and Sicily* (Oxford 1967)
LCS Suppl.II	A.D. Trendall, *The Red-Figured Vases of Lucania, Campania and Sicily, Supplement II* (*BICS* Suppl. 31, London 1973)
LCS Suppl.III	A.D. Trendall, *The Red-Figured Vases of Lucania, Campania and Sicily, Supplement III* (*BICS* Suppl. 41, London 1983)
LIMC	*Lexicon Iconographicum Mythologiae Classicae*, Zurich–Munich, i (1981), ii (1984), iii (1986), iv (1988), v (1990), vi (1992)
Marshall, *Jewellery*	F.H. Marshall, *Catalogue of the Jewellery, Greek, Etruscan, and Roman in the Departments of Antiquities, British Museum* (London, 1911, repr. 1969)
MMC³	T.B.L. Webster, *Monuments Illustrating Old and Middle Comedy*, 3rd edn, revised and enlarged by J.R. Green (*BICS* Suppl. 39, London 1978)
MNC³	T.B.L. Webster, *Monuments Illustrating New Comedy* (third edn, rev. and en. by J.R. Green and Axel Seeberg, *BICS* Suppl. 50, forthcoming)

MTS[2]	T.B.L. Webster, *Monuments Illustrating Tragedy and Satyr-Play*[2] (*BICS* Suppl. 20, London 1967)
NumAntCl	*Numismatica ed Antichità Classiche. Quaderni Ticinesi*
PhV[2]	A.D. Trendall, *Phlyax Vases* (second edn, *BICS* Suppl. 19, London 1967) [new edition forthcoming]
Pickard-Cambridge, *Dithyramb*	A.W. Pickard-Cambridge, *Dithyramb, Tragedy and Comedy* ([1]Oxford 1927, [2]rev. T.B.L. Webster, Oxford 1962)
Pickard-Cambridge, *Festivals*	A.W. Pickard-Cambridge, *The Dramatic Festivals of Athens* ([1]Oxford 1953, [2]rev. John Gould and D.M. Lewis, Oxford 1968, reissue with supplement and corrections, Oxford 1988)
Ridgway, *Hell.Sc.*	B.S. Ridgway, *Hellenistic Sculpture I: The Styles of ca. 331–200 B.C.* (Madison, Wis. 1990)
RVAp	A.D. Trendall and A. Cambitoglou, *The Red-Figured Vases of Apulia*, i (Oxford 1978), ii (Oxford 1982)
RVAp Suppl.	A.D. Trendall and A. Cambitoglou, *The Red-Figured Vases of Apulia, Supplement I* (*BICS* Suppl. 42, London 1983); *Supplement II* (*BICS* Suppl. 60, London 1991)
RVP	A.D. Trendall, *The Red-Figured Vases of Paestum* (London 1987)
RVSIS	A.D. Trendall, *Red Figure Vases of South Italy and Sicily* (London 1989)
Séchan	L. Séchan, *Etudes sur la tragédie grecque dans ses rapports avec la céramique* (Paris 1926, repr. 1967)
Walters, *Bronzes*	H.B. Walters, *Catalogue of the Bronzes, Greek, Roman, and Etruscan, in the Department of Greek and Roman Antiquities* (London 1899)
Walters, *Gems*	H.B. Walters, *Catalogue of the Engraved Gems and Cameos Greek Etruscan and Roman in the British Museum* (revised edn, London 1926)
Walters, *Lamps*	H.B. Walters, *Catalogue of the Greek and Roman Lamps in the British Museum* (London, 1914)
Walters, *Terracottas*	H.B. Walters, *Catalogue of the Terracottas in the Department of Greek and Roman Antiquities* (London 1903)
Webster, *GTP*	*Greek Theatre Production* (London [1]1956, [2]1970)
Webster, *Hell. Art*	T.B.L. Webster, *Hellenistic Art* (London 1967)

Select Bibliography

This is a short select list from a very large number of books and articles on the Greek theatre in English and several other major languages: the survey by Green (*Lustrum* 31, 1989) of publications concerned with theatre production for the years 1971–1986 dealt with 670 items, and the sequel now being prepared shows no sign that the pace has slackened. For an introduction to the subject, we would recommend Simon, or (now dated in parts) Webster's *Greek Theatre Production* or Gould (the section on Drama in the *Cambridge History of Classical Literature* has compact discussions of all the major playwrights, and was published separately in 1989). Pickard-Cambridge's three books remain standard works of reference in their subjects; Bieber, with her 870 illustrations, is still the most copious single source of plates, but should be used with some caution. For both special and general interest, we cordially commend the collections of essays by Knox and those edited by Winkler and Zeitlin, by Sommerstein and others and by Scodel.

More specialist references, particularly to the objects as objects, will be found in the bibliographies of individual items in the Catalogue.

M. Bieber, *The History of the Greek and Roman Theater* (2nd edn, Princeton 1961)

W.R. Connor, 'City Dionysia and Athenian Democracy', *Classica et Mediaevalia* 40, 1989, 7–32

E. Csapo and W.J. Slater, *The Context of Greek Theater* (Ann Arbor 1994)

C.W. Dearden, *The Stage of Aristophanes* (London 1975)

G.E. Duckworth, *The Nature of Roman Comedy* (1st edn, Princeton 1952; 2nd edn, with a Foreword and Bibliographical Appendix by Richard Hunter, Bristol 1994)

G.F. Else, *The Origin and Early Form of Greek Tragedy* (Martin Classical Lectures, 20, Cambridge, Mass. 1965)

E. Fantham, 'Roman Experience of Menander in the Late Republic and Early Empire', *Transactions & Proceedings of the American Philological Association* 114, 1984, 299–310

B. Gentili, *Theatrical Performances in the Ancient World: Hellenistic and Early Roman Theatre* (London 1979)

J. Gould, 'Greek Tragedy in Performance', *Cambridge History of Classical Literature* i (1985) 263–281

J.R. Green, 'A Representation of the *Birds* of Aristophanes', *Greek Vases in the J. Paul Getty Museum* 2 (1985) 95–118

— 'Greek Theatre Production, 1971–1986', *Lustrum* 31, 1989, 7–95, and 273–278

— 'On Seeing and Depicting the Theatre in Classical Athens', *GRBS* 32, 1991, 15–50

— *Theatre in Greek Society* (London 1994)

E.W. Handley, 'The Conventions of the Comic Stage and their Exploitation by Menander', (in) E.G. Turner (ed.), *Ménandre (Entretiens Hardt* xvi, Vandœuvres-Geneva 1970) 1–42

— 'Plautus and his Public: Some Thoughts on New Comedy in Latin', *Dioniso* 46, 1975, 117–132

— 'Comedy. From Aristophanes to Menander',

Cambridge History of Classical Literature i (1985) 398–414

— 'Aristophanes and his Theatre', (in) J.M. Bremer and E.W. Handley (eds), *Aristophane* (*Entretiens Hardt* xxxviii, Vandœuvres-Geneva 1993) 97–123

B. Hunningher, *Acoustics and Acting in the Theatre of Dionysus Eleuthereus* (1956: Mededelingen der k. Nederlandse Ak. van Wetenschappen, afd. Letterkunde, N.R., Deel 19, No. 9)

B. Knox, *Word and Action. Essays on the Ancient Theatre* (Baltimore 1979)

K. Neiiendam, *The Art of Acting in Antiquity* (Copenhagen, 1992)

A.W. Pickard-Cambridge, *The Theatre of Dionysus in Athens* (Oxford 1946)

— *Dithyramb, Tragedy and Comedy* (2nd edn rev. by T.B.L. Webster, Oxford 1962)

— *The Dramatic Festivals of Athens* (2nd edn by J. Gould and D.M. Lewis, 1968, reissued with supplement and corrections, Oxford 1988)

E. Rawson, 'Theatrical Life in Republican Rome and Italy', *Papers of the British School at Rome* 53, 1985, 97–113

R. Rehm, *Greek Tragic Theatre* (London–New York, 1992)

C.F. Russo, *Aristophanes: An Author for the Stage* (London 1994)

R. Scodel (ed.), *Theater and Society in the Classical World* (Ann Arbor, 1993)

A. Seeberg, *Corinthian Komos Vases* (*BICS* Suppl. 27, London 1971)

G.M. Sifakis, *Studies in the History of Hellenistic Drama* (London 1967)

— *Parabasis and Animal Choruses* (London 1971)

E. Simon, *The Ancient Theatre* (London 1982)

A.H. Sommerstein *et al.* (eds), *Tragedy, Comedy and the Polis. Papers from the Greek Drama Conference, Nottingham, 18–20 July 1990* (Bari 1993)

O. Taplin, *The Stagecraft of Aeschylus. Observations on the Dramatic Use of Exits & Entrances* (Oxford 1977)

— *Comic Angels and Other Approaches to Greek Drama through Vase-Paintings* (Oxford 1993)

A.D. Trendall and T.B.L. Webster, *Illustrations of Greek Drama* (London 1971)

P. Walcot, *Greek Drama in its Theatrical and Social Context* (Cardiff 1976)

T.B.L. Webster, *The Greek Chorus* (London 1970)

— *Greek Theatre Production* (2nd edn, London 1970)

— *Studies in Later Greek Comedy* (2nd edn, Manchester 1970)

— *An Introduction to Menander* (Manchester 1974)

D. Wiles, *The Masks of Menander. Sign and Meaning in Greek and Roman Performances* (Cambridge 1991)

J.J. Winkler and F.I.Zeitlin (eds), *Nothing to Do with Dionysos? Athenian Drama in its Social Context* (Princeton 1990)

Index of Museum Numbers

Index of Authors and Texts Referred to